BUILDING VOCABULARY SKILLS *SHORT VERSION*

Donald J. Goodman
MUSKEGON COMMUNITY COLLEGE

Carole Mohr

TOWNSEND PRESS   Marlton, NJ 08053

The Seven Books in the Townsend Press Vocabulary Series:

GROUNDWORK FOR A BETTER VOCABULARY
BUILDING VOCABULARY SKILLS
IMPROVING VOCABULARY SKILLS
ADVANCING VOCABULARY SKILLS
BUILDING VOCABULARY SKILLS, SHORT VERSION
IMPROVING VOCABULARY SKILLS, SHORT VERSION
ADVANCING VOCABULARY SKILLS, SHORT VERSION

Supplements Available for Each Book:

Instructor's Manual and Test Bank
Set of Computer Disks

For information on any of these books or supplements,
or other books on the Townsend Press reading list,
write to the address shown below.

Townsend Press, Inc.
Pavilions at Greentree—408
Marlton, New Jersey 08053
609-772-6410

Send books orders and requests for desk copies or supplements to:

Townsend Press Book Center
RD # 11, Box 192A
Mt. Penn Road
Reading, PA 19607
1-215-796-0929
FAX 1-215-796-1491

ISBN 0-944210-82-1

Contents

Note: For ease of reference, the title of the passage that concludes each chapter appears in parentheses.

UNIT FOUR

Appendixes

Preface

The problem is all too familiar: *students just don't know enough words*. Reading, writing, and content teachers agree that many students' vocabularies are inadequate to the demands of courses. Weak vocabularies limit students' understanding of what they read and the clarity and depth of what they write.

The purpose of the Townsend Press vocabulary series is to provide a solid, workable answer to the vocabulary problem. The short version of the series consists of three books, each of which *teaches* 160 important words. Within each book are 20 chapters, with 8 words in each chapter. Here are the distinctive features of BUILDING VOCABULARY SKILLS, SHORT VERSION:

1 An intensive words-in-context approach. Studies show that students learn words best by seeing them repeatedly in different contexts, not through rote memorization. BUILDING VOCABULARY SKILLS, SHORT VERSION, gives students an intensive in-context experience by presenting each word in seven different contexts. Each chapter takes students through a productive sequence of steps:

- Students first see a word in a preview.
- They then infer the meaning of the word by considering two sentences in which it appears.
- Based on their inferences, students select and confirm each word's meaning in a matching test. They are then in a solid position to further strengthen their knowledge oi a word.
- Finally, they strengthen their knowledge of a word by applying it three times: in two sentence practices and in a passage practice.

Each encounter with a word brings it closer to becoming part of the student's permanent word bank.

2 Abundant practice. In addition to the extensive practice in each chapter, there are *four unit tests* at the end of each five-chapter unit. These tests reinforce students' knowledge of every word in every chapter. Further, there are added tests in the *Test Bank* and the *computer disks* that accompany the book. All this practice means that students learn in the surest possible way: by working closely and repeatedly with each word.

3 Controlled feedback. Students receive feedback on two of the practices in each vocabulary chapter. A limited answer key at the back of the book lets them see how they did with the opening preview of words. The key also provides answers for the first sentence check in the chapter. The key enables students to take an active role in their own learning. And they are likely to use the answer key in an honest and positive way if they know they may be tested on the many activities and selections for which answers are not provided. (Answers not in the book are in the Instructor's Manual. They can, of course, be copied from the manual and passed out at the teacher's discretion.)

4 Focus on essential words. A good deal of time and research went into selecting the 160 words featured in the book. Word frequency lists were consulted, along with lists in a wide number of vocabulary books. In addition, the authors and editors each prepared their own lists. A computer was used to help in the consolidation of the many word lists. A long process of group discussion then led to final decisions about the words that would be more helpful for students on a basic reading level.

5 Appealing content. Dull practice materials work against learning. On the other hand, meaningful, lively, and at times even funny sentences and passages can spark students' attention and thus encourage their grasp of the material. For this reason, a great deal of effort was put into creating sentences and passages with both widespread appeal *and* solid context support. We have tried throughout to make the practice materials truly enjoyable for teachers and students alike. Look, for example, at the passage on page 8 that closes the first chapter of this book.

6 Clarity of format. The book has been designed so that its very format contributes to the learning process. All eight words of a chapter appear on a single page, and each practice begins and ends on one page. In particular, each chapter has a two-page spread (turn, for example, to pages 6-7) so that students can refer to the eight words in context on one side while working on the matching test and sentence check on the other side. And a second color has been used within the book to help make the content as visually appealing as possible.

7 Supplementary materials.

a A combined *Instructor's Manual and Test Bank* is available at no charge to instructors using the book. It can be obtained by writing to the Reading Editor, Townsend Press, Pavilions at Greentree—408, Marlton, NJ 08053. This booklet contains pre- and post-tests for all four units in the text as well as teaching suggestions, a model syllabus, an answer key, and a set of mastery tests for each chapter.

b A *comprehensive series of computer disks* also accompanies the book. These disks provide four tests for each of the 20 vocabulary chapters. The disks are self-booting and contain a number of other user- and instructor-friendly features, including brief explanations of answers, a sound option, frequent mention of the user's first name, a running score at the bottom of the screen, and a record-keeping file.

Probably in no other area of reading instruction is the computer more useful than in reinforcing vocabulary. This vocabulary program takes full advantage of the computer's unique capabilities and motivational appeal. Here's how the program works:

- Students are tested on the eight words in a chapter, with each word in a sentence context different from any in the book itself.
- After students answer each question, they receive immediate feedback: The computer tells if a student is right or wrong and *why*, frequently using the student's first name and providing a running score.
- When the test is over, the computer supplies a test score and—this especially is what is unique about this program—a chance to retest on the specific words the student got wrong. For example, if a student misses four items on a test, the retest provides *four different sentences* that test just those four words. Students then receive a score for this special retest. What is so valuable about this, of course, is that the computer gives students added practice in the words they most need to review.
- In addition, the computer offers a *second*, more challenging test in which students must identify the meanings of the chapter words without benefit of context. This test is a final check that students have really learned the words. And, again, there is the option of a retest, tailor-made to recheck only those words missed on the first definition test.

By the end of this program, students' knowledge of each word in the chapter will have been carefully reinforced. And this reinforcement will be the more effective for having occurred in an electronic medium that especially engages today's students.

A demo disk will be sent to any teacher requesting it. The full set of disks, with unlimited copying privileges, will be available at no charge to departments adopting at least 200 copies of the book.

8 Realistic pricing. We wanted a book that would offer the highest possible quality at the best possible price. We are delighted that Townsend Press has committed to sell this book to students at a price under nine dollars. Such a modest price makes it an inexpensive supplement for any reading or writing course.

9 One in a sequence of books. BUILDING VOCABULARY SKILLS, SHORT VERSION, is the basic text in a sequence that includes IMPROVING VOCABULARY SKILLS, SHORT VERSION (an intermediate text) and ADVANCING VOCABULARY SKILLS, SHORT VERSION (a more advanced text). Suggested grade levels for each book are included in the *Instructor's Manual*. Together, the three books will help create a vocabulary foundation that will make any student a better reader, writer, and thinker.

Acknowledgments

Our thanks go to the talented group of writers and editors at Townsend Press who have worked closely with us on the book: John Langan, Joan Dunayer, Jane Mackay, and Beth Johnson Ruth. We also acknowledge the extraordinary programming efforts of Professor Terry Hutchison of Atlantic Community College. He has helped us create exactly the kind of sophisticated, comprehensive software that we believe is needed to solidify students' learning of all the words in the book. Inspiration for the cover came from an idea by Janet M. Goldstein, and the cover itself owes thanks to the artistry of Larry Didona. We appreciate as well the customized page design work of Alysse Einbender, and we are particularly grateful for the design, editing, and proofreading skills of Janet M. Goldstein.

Donald J. Goodman   *Carole Mohr*

Introduction

WHY VOCABULARY DEVELOPMENT COUNTS

You have probably often heard it said, "Building vocabulary is important." Maybe you've politely nodded in agreement and then forgotten the matter. But it would be fair for you to ask, "Why *is* vocabulary development important? Provide some evidence." Here are four compelling kinds of evidence.

1   Common sense tells you what many research studies have shown as well: vocabulary is a basic part of reading comprehension. Simply put, if you don't know enough words, you are going to have trouble understanding what you read. An occasional word may not stop you, but if there are too many words you don't know, comprehension will suffer. The *content* of textbooks is often challenge enough; you don't want to work as well on understanding the *words* that make up that content.

2   Vocabulary is a major part of almost every standardized test, including reading achievement tests, college entrance exams, and armed forces and vocational placement tests. Test authors know that vocabulary is a key measure of both one's learning and one's ability to learn. So they have a separate vocabulary section as well as a reading comprehension section. The more words you know, then, the better you are likely to do on such important tests.

3   Studies have made clear that students with strong vocabularies are more successful in school. And one widely known study found that a good vocabulary, more than any other factor, was common to people enjoying successful careers in life. Words are in fact the tools not just of better reading, but of writing, speaking, listening, and thinking as well. The more words you have at your command, the more effective your communication can be, and the more influence you can have on the people around you.

4   In the world of the 1990s, a good vocabulary will count more than ever. Far fewer people will work on farms or in factories. Far more will be in jobs that provide services or process information. More than ever, words will be the tools of our trade: words we use in reading, writing, listening, and speaking. Furthermore, experts say that workers of the 90s will be called on to change jobs and learn new skills at an ever-increasing pace. The keys to survival and success will thus be the abilities to communicate skillfully and learn quickly. A solid vocabulary is essential for both of these skills.

The evidence is overwhelming, then, that building vocabulary is crucial. The question then becomes, "What is the best way of going about it?"

1

WORDS IN CONTEXT: THE KEY TO VOCABULARY DEVELOPMENT

Memorizing lists of words is a traditional method of vocabulary development. But a person is likely to forget such memorized lists quickly. Studies show that to master a word you must see and use it in various contexts. By working actively and repeatedly with a word, you greatly increase the chance of really learning it.

The following activity will make clear how the book is organized and how it uses a words-in-context approach. Answer the questions or fill in the missing words in the spaces provided.

Contents

Turn to the table of contents on pages iii-iv.

• How many chapters are in the book? _____

• Three short sections follow the chapters. The first provides a limited answer key; the second gives helpful information on using _____; and the third is an index of the 160 words in the book.

Vocabulary Chapters

Turn to Chapter 1 on pages 5-8. This chapter, like all the others, consists of six parts:

• The *first part*, on page 5, is titled _____

This preview introduces you to the eight words covered in the chapter. After you try filling in the blanks, you are asked to check the _____ at the back and to fill in any empty blanks.

• The *second part* of the chapter, on page 6, is titled _____

The left-hand column lists the eight words. Under each word is its _____ (in parentheses) and its part of speech (*noun, verb,* or *adjective*). For example, we are told that *acknowledge,* the first word on page 6, is a verb.

Using the pronunciation guide requires only a bit of information: Short vowels have no special mark, while long vowels are indicated with a line above the vowel. (Note that long vowels have the sound of their own name.) What is the first word in the list with a long vowel? _____ . Symbols that sound like "uh"—like the "uh" a speaker makes when hesitating—are symbolized by the schwa (ə), which looks like an upside down *e.* What is the first word in the list with a schwa? _____. Finally, an accent mark (') tells which syllable to emphasize when pronouncing a word. What is the first word in the list with an accent on the second syllable? _____ A brief guide to the dictionary on page 120 gives further information on pronouncing words.

To the right of each word are two sentences that help you understand its meaning. In each sentence, the *context* —the words surrounding the boldfaced word—provides clues you can use to figure out the definition. For example, look at the first sentence for the word *acknowledge.*

Andrea was annoyed when Hal used one of her jokes in his class speech without **acknowledging** that the joke was hers.

Based on the context, what is the meaning of *acknowledging*?

     a. hiding   b. wishing   c. admitting   d. denying

A second sentence also helps you pin down the meaning:

Even when the votes were counted, Senator Rice refused to **acknowledge** that he had lost.

By looking closely at each pair of sentences, you can decide on the meaning of a word. (In the example above, *acknowledging* clearly means *admitting*.) As you figure out each meaning, you are working actively with the word. You are creating the groundwork you need to understand *and* to remember the word. Getting involved with the word and developing a feel for it, based upon its use in context, is the key to word mastery.

It is with good reason, then, that the directions at the top of page 6 tell you to look _____ and _____ at the context. Doing so deepens your sense of the word and prepares you for the next activity.

• The *third part* of the chapter, on page 7, is titled _____.

According to research, it is not enough to see a word in context. At a certain point, it is important as well to see the meaning of a word. The matching test provides that meaning, but it also makes you look for and think about that meaning. In other words, it continues the active learning that is your surest route to learning and remembering a word.

Note the caution that follows the test. Do not proceed any further until you are sure that you know the correct meaning of each word.

• The *fourth part* of the chapter (also on page 7) is titled _____.

Here are eight sentences that give you an opportunity to apply your understanding of the eight words. After inserting the words, check your answers in the limited key at the back of the book. Be sure to use the answer key as a learning tool only. Doing so will help you to master the words and to prepare for the last two activities and the unit tests, for which answers are not provided.

• The *fifth part* of the chapter, on page 8, is titled _____ , and the *sixth part* is titled _____.

Both practices test you on all eight words, giving you a chance to deepen your mastery. In the second activity, you have the context of an entire passage in which you can practice and apply the words.

At the bottom of the last page of this chapter is a box where you can enter your score for the final two checks. These scores should also be entered into the vocabulary performance chart located on the inside back page of the book. To get your score, all you need do is to refer to the following scale, which appears on the last page of every chapter:

> 0 wrong = 100%
> 1 wrong = 88%
> 2 wrong = 75%
> 3 wrong = 63%
> 4 wrong = 50%
> and so on.

You now know, in a nutshell, how to proceed with the words in each chapter. Make sure that you do each page very carefully. *Remember, as you work through the activities, you are learning the words.*

How many times in all will you use each word? If you look, you'll see that each chapter gives you the opportunity to work with each word seven times. Each "impression" adds to the likelihood that the word will become part of your active vocabulary. You will have further opportunities to use the word in the four unit tests that follow each chapter and on the computer disks that are available with the book.

FINAL THOUGHTS

The facts are in. A strong vocabulary is a source of power. Words can make you a better reader, writer, speaker, thinker, and learner. They can dramatically increase your chances of success in school and in your job.

But words will not come automatically. They must be learned in a program of regular study. If you commit yourself to learning words, and you work actively and honestly with the chapters in this book, you will not only enrich your vocabulary—you will enrich your life as well.

Previewing the Words

Find out how many of the eight words in this chapter you already know. Try to complete each sentence with the most suitable word from the list below. Use each word once.

Leave a sentence blank rather than guessing at an answer. Your purpose here is just to get a sense of the eight words and what you may know about them.

acknowledge	alternative	appropriate	candid
compel	comply	concise	drastic

1. People do not always support _____ changes in fashion, such as extreme shifts in hem lines.

2. Though Rita had asked Jack for his _____ opinion, she was still hurt when he criticized her paper.

3. Our boss expects us to _____ with his instructions without asking questions or pointing out problems.

4. People often find it difficult to _____ their errors. They hate to admit they were wrong.

5. When you go on a job interview, it is _____ to dress as you would if you had the position you're interviewing for.

6. Dale's poor grades left him with two _____s—to work fewer hours at his part-time job or to drop a class.

7. My history teacher would often _____ us to do useless work, such as memorizing the date each state entered the union.

8. Answers to essay questions should be _____. Often students waste test time by writing wordy answers that don't say much.

Now check your answers by turning to page 117. Fix any mistakes and fill in any blank spaces by writing in the correct answers. By doing so, you will complete this introduction to the eight words.

You're now ready to strengthen your knowledge of the words you already know and to master the words you're only half sure of, or don't know at all. Turn to the next page.

Eight Words in Context

Figure out the meanings of the following eight words by looking *closely and carefully* at the context in which the words appear. Doing so will prepare you for the matching test and the practices on the two pages that follow.

1 **acknowledge**
(ak-nol'-ij)
-*verb*

   a. Andrea was annoyed when Hal used one of her jokes in his class speech without **acknowledging** that the joke was hers.

   b. Even when the votes were counted, Senator Rice refused to **acknowledge** he had lost.

2 **alternative**
(ôl-tûr'-nə-tiv)
-*noun*

   a. The teacher stated the **alternatives** to Tim—retake the test or get a D for the course.

   b. When her dog clearly began to suffer from cancer, Inez felt she had no **alternative**. It was necessary to have him put to sleep.

3 **appropriate**
(ə-pro'-prē-it)
-*adjective*

   a. Chuck has little sense of what is socially **appropriate**. For example, he went to his sister's wedding in jogging shoes.

   b. In a church it is considered **appropriate** for a man to take his hat off, but in a synagogue it is considered proper for a man to cover his head.

4 **candid**
(kan'-did)
-*adjective*

   a. A child is a striking combination of boldfaced liar ("I didn't eat the cookie") and painfully **candid** reporter ("Gee, you've gotten really fat").

   b. Many people admire David's open, **candid** nature; others consider him too outspoken.

5 **compel**
(kəm-pel')
-*verb*

   a. It is a sad sight to see the crack of a whip **compel** a grand cat like the lion to leap through hoops for a crowd's amusement.

   b. You can **compel** a weaker person to obey, but you can never force someone to feel respect.

6 **comply**
(kəm-plī')
-*verb*

   a. If someone with an iron pipe demands your wallet, it is safer to **comply** than to resist.

   b. My husband is so used to being boss at work that he is annoyed when I don't **comply** with his every request at home.

7 **concise**
(kon-sīs')
-*adjective*

   a. Journalists tend to write very **concise** prose because a newspaper column offers limited space.

   b. Unlike many politicians, our mayor is **concise**—his speeches are short but say much.

8 **drastic**
(dras'-tik)
-*adjective*

   a. The new president of Super Steel Products took **drastic** steps, closing two factories and laying off 300 employees.

   b. "This time I will let you off with just an hour after school," the principal said. "But if it happens again, the punishment will be more **drastic**."

Matching Words and Definitions

Check your understanding of the eight words by matching each word with its definition. Look back at the sentences in "Eight Words in Context" as needed to decide on the meaning of each word.

_e_	1. **acknowledge**	a.	to do as commanded or asked
_c_	2. **alternative**	b.	proper; suitable to the situation
_b_	3. **appropriate**	c.	a choice
____	4. **candid**	d.	extreme; harsh or intense
_f_	5. **compel**	e.	to confess or admit
_a_	6. **comply**	f.	to force
_h_	7. **concise**	g.	very honest
_d_	8. **drastic**	h.	communicating much in a few clear words

CAUTION: Do not go any further until you are sure the above answers are correct. If you have studied the "Eight Words in Context," you will know how to match each word. Then you can use the matches to help you in the following practices. Your goal is to reach a point where you don't need to check definitions at all.

Sentence Check 1

Complete each sentence below with the most suitable word from the box. Use each word once.

acknowledge	alternative	appropriate	candid
compel	comply	concise	drastic

1. Because Frank seems so _____, everyone believes him even when he tells a lie.

2. People often take _____ steps in anger, extreme actions that they later regret.

3. In traditional wedding ceremonies, the clergy person is often wordy, while the bride and groom are very

   _____.

4. Many Americans do not fully _____ with the tax rules of this country.

5. A couple of older boys tried to _____ some first graders to hand over their lunch money.

6. After high school, Kenny felt his _____s were either to join the military or to get a job. Then, when he had saved enough money, he could go to college.

7. When the real ax-murderer confessed, the police had to _____ that the wrong man had been jailed.

8. In most American schools, it is not _____ for students to call their teachers by their first names.

Now check your answers to these questions by turning to page 117. Going over the answers carefully will help you prepare for the next two checks, for which answers are not given.

➤ Sentence Check 2

Complete each sentence below with two words from the following list. Use each word once.

acknowledge	alternative	appropriate	candid
compel	comply	concise	drastic

1-2. The sale sign was huge but _____—it said only, "_____ price cuts."

3-4. In colonial America, it was thought _____ for wives to _____ with all their husbands' commands.

5-6. "The poor economic situation leaves me no _____," said the company president. "It _____s me to lay off some of our workers."

7-8. "I _____ that you have a perfect right to do whatever you like with your hair," said the teenage girl's mother. "But, to be _____, I don't find green curls attractive."

➤ Final Check: Taking Exams

Here is a final opportunity for you to strengthen your knowledge of the eight words. First read the following passage carefully. Then fill in each blank with a word from the box at the top of this page. (Context clues will help you figure out which word goes in which blank.) Use each word once.

There are four test-taking methods to consider when faced with exams. The first is to impress your teachers with very clever answers. For example, you might respond to any question beginning with the word "why" with a simple, (1)_____ "Why not?" This is not recommended, however, unless you know an instructor has great respect for humor. A second method is simply to refuse to take an exam. You might try writing something like, "This is a free country, so you can't (2)_____ me to take this test. Besides, I partied all last night." This method should not be used unless you are in (3)_____ need, as it involves a great deal of risk. It is (4)_____ only if you have shown yourself to be very brilliant throughout the course and you are the teacher's pet. Otherwise, you can expect your teacher simply to refuse to pass you. A third way of dealing with a test is to (5)_____ly admit helplessness. The story is told of a student who openly (6)_____(e)d ignorance by writing, "God only knows the answer to this question." Unfortunately, the instructor's response was, "God gets an A. You get an F." So to avoid failure, you usually have no (7)_____—you must (8)_____ with school rules. The final method for dealing with college exams, then, is clear: learn the material.

SCORES: Sentence Check 2 _____ %		Final Check _____ %

Enter your scores above and in the vocabulary performance chart on the inside back cover of the book.

Number right: 8 = 100%   7 = 88%   6 = 75%   5 = 63%   4 = 50%   3 = 38%   2 = 25%   1 = 13%

Previewing the Words

Find out how many of the eight words in this chapter you already know. Try to complete each sentence with the most suitable word from the list below. Use each word once.

Leave a sentence blank rather than guessing at an answer. Your purpose here is just to get a sense of the eight words and what you may know about them.

erratic ²	extensive ⁵	fortify ³	⁶ illuminate
⁷ isolate	refuge ⁸	reminisce ⁴	urban ¹

1. Just as the cockroach annoys _____ dwellers, the mosquito pesters people in the country and suburbs.

2. Tina's test scores are _____—sometimes she scores very high, other times very low.

3. Babies need milk to _____ their bones.

4. My grandmother likes to _____ about her childhood in Ireland.

5. Jackie did _____ research for her paper by reading many books and articles.

6. During the power failure, Leslie used a battery-operated lamp to _____ the living room.

7. Some people _____ themselves when they are unhappy. Others seek the company of friends and family.

8. My wife and I first met when we took _____ in the same doorway during a sudden rain.

Now check your answers by turning to page 117. Fix any mistakes and fill in any blank spaces by writing in the correct answers. By doing so, you will complete this introduction to the eight words.

You're now ready to strengthen your knowledge of the words you already know and to master the words you're only half sure of, or don't know at all. Turn to the next page.

Eight Words in Context

Figure out the meanings of the following eight words by looking *closely and carefully* at the context in which the words appear. Doing so will prepare you for the matching test and the practices on the two pages that follow.

1 **erratic**
(i-rat'-ik)
-adjective

  a. My son's eating habits are **erratic.** One day he'll barely eat, and the next he'll eat enough for three.

  b. The driver ahead of me was **erratic**—he kept changing his speed and his lane.

2 **extensive**
(ek-sten'-siv)
-adjective

  a. John dislikes mowing grass, so he has only a small yard instead of an **extensive** lawn.

  b. To save the wounded police officer, doctors performed **extensive** surgery that lasted for hours.

3 **fortify**
(fôr'-tə-fī')
-verb

  a. The night before running a marathon, Elsa **fortifies** herself by eating a large plate of pasta.

  b. The builders planned to **fortify** the old tower with steel beams.

4 **illuminate**
(i-lōō'-mə-nāt')
-verb

  a. Before electricity, streets were **illuminated** by gaslight.

  b. On Halloween, we made our trick-or-treat rounds with a flashlight to **illuminate** the way.

5 **isolate**
(ī'-sə-lāt')
-verb

  a. I thought I would enjoy **isolating** myself at the vacation cabin, but I soon felt lonely.

  b. Freddy was such a troublemaker that the teacher put his desk in a far corner to **isolate** him from the other students.

6 **refuge**
(ref-yōōj)
-noun

  a. A motorcycle offers no **refuge** in bad weather.

  b. In *The Wizard of Oz*, Dorothy doesn't reach the storm cellar in time to take **refuge** from the tornado.

7 **reminisce**
(rem'-ə-nis')
-verb

  a. On their wedding anniversary, Lenny and Jean **reminisced** about their first date.

  b. My father showed me his trophy and **reminisced** about his years as a star basketball player.

8 **urban**
(ur'-bən)
-adjective

  a. Skyscrapers make for tightly packed **urban** populations. For example, some 35,000 people work in the twin towers of the World Trade Center in New York City.

  b. Gladys likes **urban** living because she grew up in the city, but Ben, who grew up on a farm, prefers country life.

Matching Words and Definitions .

Check your understanding of the eight words by matching each word with its definition. Look back at the sentences in "Eight Words in Context" as needed to decide on the meaning of each word.

_h_ 1. **erratic**   a. to light up

_e_ 2. **extensive**   b. shelter; protection

_f_ 3. **fortify**   c. of or in a city

_a_ 4. **illuminate**   d. to separate from others

_d_ 5. **isolate**   e. large in space or amount

___ 6. **refuge**   f. to strengthen

___ 7. **reminisce**   g. to remember and talk about the past

___ 8. **urban**   h. not consistent

> CAUTION: Do not go any further until you are sure the above answers are correct. If you have studied the "Eight Words in Context," you will know how to match each word. Then you can use the matches to help you in the following practices. Your goal is to reach a point where you don't need to check definitions at all.

➤ Sentence Check 1

Complete each sentence below with the most suitable word from the box. Use each word once.

erratic	extensive	fortify	illuminate
isolate	refuge	reminisce	urban

1. The skater's _____ performances showed she was too inconsistent to hire for the ice show.

2. In London during World War II, bomb shelters provided _____ from air attacks.

3. Vitamins and minerals _____ the body against disease.

4. Criminals are put in prison to _____ them from the rest of society.

5. The night before graduation, Gary and I _____(e)d about our four years together.

6. The pioneers used candles to _____ book pages at night.

7. Before his parents visit him, Don gives his apartment a(n) _____ cleaning—dusting or scrubbing every surface.

8. There's a big difference between a(n) _____ sky and a country sky. In the country, there are no bright lights to overpower the starlight.

Now check your answers to these questions by turning to page 117. Going over the answers carefully will help you prepare for the next two checks, for which answers are not given.

➤ *Sentence Check 2*

Complete each sentence below with two words from the following list. Use each word once.

erratic	extensive	fortify	illuminate
isolate	refuge	reminisce	urban

1-2. The loud celebrating on the Fourth of July is so _____ in my neighborhood that the

only place I find _____ from the noise is in my basement.

3-4. Curt _____(e)d for hours, revealing that his life had been very_____.
At some points in his life, he was very busy, married, and well off. At other times, he lived alone and
was out of work.

5-6. Cities could reduce _____ crime if they would _____ streets and
playgrounds with brighter lights, since criminals work in the shadows.

7-8. To keep the opposing army from trying to _____ his weaker force from the rest of the

unit, the general decided to _____ his defenses.

➤ *Final Check:* Nate the Woodsman

Here is a final opportunity for you to strengthen your knowledge of the eight words. First read the following passage carefully. Then fill in each blank with a word from the box at the top of this page. (Context clues will help you figure out which word goes in which blank.) Use each word once.

Nate had spent most of his 70 years in the woods. (1)_____ life was not for
him. He preferred to (2)_____ himself from others and find (3)_____
in nature from the crowds and noise of the city. He was more than willing to give up such advantages
as flush toilets and electric blankets for the joy of watching a sunrise (4)_____ the
frozen pines.

Living so alone as he did made him (5)_____. For example, one minute he'd
be tight-lipped, and the next he'd (6)_____ at length about his youth. His
knowledge of nature was (7)_____, and so I learned much from him over the years.

One event shows how wise he was about the woods and how miserly he could be with words.
One evening Nate, my cousin Arthur, and I were crossing a meadow filled with little white
mushrooms.

"Those mushrooms look so good," said Arthur. "Did you ever use them, Nate?"

"Yep," said Nate. "My ma used to cook 'em up."

"Great!" said Arthur. Nate's words seemed to (8)_____ Arthur's desire for
those mushrooms. He gathered about a hundred of them. "How'd she fix them?" he asked Nate.

"Cooked 'em up with sugar water."

"Really? And then you ate them that way?"

"Ate 'em?" Nate was horrified. "You crazy? We used to put 'em in a bowl on the table to kill
flies!"

SCORES: Sentence Check 2 _____ % Final Check _____ %
Enter your scores above and in the vocabulary performance chart on the inside back cover of the book.

Number right: 8 = 100% 7 = 88% 6 = 75% 5 = 63% 4 = 50% 3 = 38% 2 = 25% 1 = 13%

Previewing the Words

Find out how many of the eight words in this chapter you already know. Try to complete each sentence with the most suitable word from the list below. Use each word once.

Leave a sentence blank rather than guessing at an answer. Your purpose here is just to get a sense of the eight words and what you may know about them.

\ impartial	legitimate⁷	lenient ⁵	₃menace
morale ₂	naive ₆	overt⁹	₄undermine

1. Is it _____ for a boss to tell a secretary to make and serve coffee? Or is it improper?

2. The team's _____ was high: they were in good spirits and thought they would win the game.

3. Ron's fast, zig-zag driving makes him a _____ on the road.

4. Tammy's late hours, bad eating habits, and chain smoking have begun to _____ her health.

5. All children like _____ babysitters who allow bedtime to be postponed an hour or two.

6. The _____ person may not survive in the inner city. It's best to be aware of all the city's dangers and how to guard against them.

7. Can a judge who has had a bitter divorce be truly _____ in a divorce trial? Or may such a judge be biased against the husband or wife in the trial?

8. Embarrassed by John's public show of affection, Kim asked him to be less

   _____ about his feelings when others were around.

Now check your answers by turning to page 117. Fix any mistakes and fill in any blank spaces by writing in the correct answers. By doing so, you will complete this introduction to the eight words.

You're now ready to strengthen your knowledge of the words you already know and to master the words you're only half sure of, or don't know at all. Turn to the next page.

Eight Words in Context

Figure out the meanings of the following eight words by looking *closely and carefully* at the context in which the words appear. Doing so will prepare you for the matching test and the practices on the two pages that follow.

1 **impartial**
(im-par'-shəl)
-*adjective*

   a. Too much pre-trial publicity makes it difficult for lawyers to find **impartial** jurors, people who have no bias about the trial.

   b. "I'm an **impartial** judge of character," Dolores joked. "I distrust all people equally, without prejudice."

2 **legitimate**
(le-jit'-ə-mit)
-*adjective*

   a. "A need to see the final episode in your favorite soap opera," said the teacher, "is not a **legitimate** excuse for missing class."

   b. Any company that guarantees to make all investors millionaires can't possibly be **legitimate.**

3 **lenient**
(lē'-nē-ənt)
-*adjective*

   a. Ms. Hall is very **lenient** about late papers. If you hand one in even a week late, she doesn't lower your grade.

   b. Mom wouldn't let us feed our poodle during dinner. But Dad, more **lenient,** would look the other way when we slipped the dog something under the table.

4 **menace**
(men'-is)
-*noun*

   a. Acid rain is the biggest **menace** to the survival of fresh-water fish.

   b. Smokey the Bear urges campers to be careful with fire, a great **menace** to forests.

5 **morale**
(mə-ral')
-*noun*

   a. Art class was good for Tyrone's **morale.** Each time the teacher praised his drawings, his confidence and enthusiasm increased.

   b. The workers' **morale** was so low that they constantly complained about the job. Only going home could cheer them up.

6 **naive**
(no-ēv')
-*adjective*

   a. Though young, Rhoda is not **naive.** Being on her own for so long has made her streetwise.

   b. Having had little experience with salespeople, my young daughter is so **naive** about them that she believes everything they tell her.

7 **overt**
(ō-vurt')
-*adjective*

   a. Sometimes **overt** racism is easier to deal with than the hidden kind. You can better fight what is out in the open.

   b. Martha's love of books was **overt**—books spilled over the shelves in every room of her apartment.

8 **undermine**
(un'-dər-mīn')
-*verb*

   a. Leroy tried to **undermine** the coach's authority by making jokes about him behind his back.

   b. Numerous floods had **undermined** the house's foundations to the extent that the house was no longer safe.

Matching Words and Definitions

Check your understanding of the eight words by matching each word with its definition. Look back at the sentences in "Eight Words in Context" as needed to decide on the meaning of each word.

_a_ 1. **impartial**   a. fair; not biased; without prejudice

_c_ 2. **legitimate**   b. a threat

_g_ 3. **lenient**   c. in accordance with law and custom; lawful or proper

_b_ 4. **menace**   d. general mood in regard to confidence and enthusiasm; spirit

_d_ 5. **morale**   e. to gradually weaken or damage

_h_ 6. **naive**   f. obvious; not hidden

_f_ 7. **overt**   g. not strict or harsh in disciplining and/or punishing; merciful

_e_ 8. **undermine**   h. lacking worldly experience; unsuspecting; unsophisticated

CAUTION: Do not go any further until you are sure the above answers are correct. If you have studied the "Eight Words in Context," you will know how to match each word. Then you can use the matches to help you in the following practices. Your goal is to reach a point where you don't need to check definitions at all.

➤ Sentence Check 1

Complete each sentence below with the most suitable word from the box. Use each word once.

impartial	legitimate	lenient	menace
morale	naive	overt	undermine

1. When my brother and I argued, my mother remained _____—she didn't want to favor either of us.

2. Alison's repeated criticisms _____d her sister's confidence.

3. Drugs have become a terrible _____ to the well-being of American children.

4. Toby's _____ was low after his operation, but he cheered up once he was allowed to get out of bed.

5. It isn't considered _____ for a 20-year-old man to date a 13-year-old girl. However, if each were ten years older, it would be perfectly proper.

6. My father is so _____ about business deals that he has been tricked by cheaters more than once.

7. Mrs. Dean's dislike for the mayor was _____. She stood right up in front of the crowd and said exactly what she thought of him.

8. "The boss is _____ about an employee's first mistake," Sherry's co-worker warned, "but he's strict about a second one."

Now check your answers to these questions by turning to page 117. Going over the answers carefully will help you prepare for the next two checks, for which answers are not given.

➤ Sentence Check 2

Complete each sentence below with two words from the following list. Use each word once.

impartial	legitimate	lenient	menace
morale	naive	overt	undermine

1-2. Nick's interest in Janice's money is _____ enough for all her friends to notice. But

Janice is so _____ that she has no idea about the real reason for Nick's attention.

3-4. The staff's _____ quickly fell when they learned that some of the company's earnings

were put into a business that was not _____ and that was being investigated by the
police.

5-6. Donald is a real _____ in the classroom. It's not uncommon for him to

_____ classroom order by snapping little spitballs at other students.

7-8. My parents should be _____, but they're much more _____ with
my sisters than with me. They often get off with a scolding, while I'm usually grounded for one or
more days.

➤ Final Check: Who's on Trial?

Here is a final opportunity for you to strengthen your knowledge of the eight words. First read the following passage carefully. Then fill in each blank with a word from the box at the top of this page. (Context clues will help you figure out which word goes in which blank.) Use each word once.

"I must be really (1)_____ about our justice system," Karen said as we left the

courtroom to get lunch. "I truly believed that if I pressed charges against that man for attacking me, he

would have a trial with a jury that would be (2)_____ enough to fairly consider all

the evidence, which would be brought out by reasonable questioning. That man is the criminal, but I

felt as if I were the one on trial. I'm ready to give up."

After sitting at the trial all morning, I could understand why Karen's (3)_____

was so low. The opposing lawyer's attempts to embarrass her and (4)_____ her

image before the jury were so (5)_____ that nobody in the courtroom could miss

them. His misleading questions about her sex life and manner of dressing were clearly meant to give

the false impression that it had been her own actions that were not (6)_____ — that

Karen "asked" to be attacked by behaving improperly. Her lawyer had gotten certain remarks

removed from the court record, but the jury had already heard things like "short skirts" and "sleep with

your boyfriend." They might jump to conclusions instead of considering the evidence. I just hoped

they would find that man guilty. I also prayed that the judge would not be

(7)_____, but would see what a (8)_____ to society this man was

and sentence him to many years in prison.

> **SCORES:**   Sentence Check 2 _____ %   **Final Check** _____ %
> Enter your scores above and in the vocabulary performance chart on the inside back cover of the book.

Previewing the Words

Find out how many of the eight words in this chapter you already know. Try to complete each sentence with the most suitable word from the list below. Use each word once.

Leave a sentence blank rather than guessing at an answer. Your purpose here is just to get a sense of the eight words and what you may know about them.

endorse	hypocrite	idealistic	illusion
impact	imply	novice	obstacle

1. The magician created the _____ that his assistant was floating upside down in midair.

2. Anita was a complete _____ when she came to work at the bank, but now she has enough experience to train new tellers.

3. The TV minister was a _____—he earned a fortune talking about how noble it is to be poor.

4. To be a radio announcer, Marla will have to overcome the _____ of her strong regional accent.

5. "I have a dream," said Martin Luther King, proud to be _____ and to have a vision of how to achieve a better world.

6. The senator refused to _____ any candidate who didn't share his views on the minimum wage.

7. When the two cars crashed into each other, the _____ was so great that one driver was thrown from his car.

8. People often _____ the question "Would you like to go out with me tonight?" by asking only, "Do you have plans for tonight?"

Now check your answers by turning to page 117. Fix any mistakes and fill in any blank spaces by writing in the correct answers. By doing so, you will complete this introduction to the eight words.

You're now ready to strengthen your knowledge of the words you already know and to master the words you're only half sure of, or don't know at all. Turn to the next page.

Eight Words in Context

Figure out the meanings of the following eight words by looking *closely and carefully* at the context in which the words appear. Doing so will prepare you for the matching test and the practices on the two pages that follow.

1 **endorse**
(en-dôrs')
-*verb*

   a. "If you **endorse** the new shopping mall," said the speaker, "you're supporting a large increase in neighborhood traffic."

   b. Some athletes earn more money **endorsing** such products as cereal and sneakers than they do playing their sport.

2 **hypocrite**
(hip'-ə-krit')
-*noun*

   a. Dominic is such a **hypocrite**. He cheats his customers while complaining to them about how hard it is to be an honest, struggling salesman.

   b. Maybe the worst **hypocrites** are those who preach love and then attack anyone of a different culture or faith.

3 **idealistic**
(i-dē'-ə-lis'-tik)
-*adjective*

   a. Very **idealistic** people are drawn to work in which they feel they can make the world a better place.

   b. My sister is too **idealistic** ever to marry for wealth or fame—she would marry only for love.

4 **illusion**
(i-lōō'-zhən)
-*noun*

   a. Rena's belief that she and Jon had a strong relationship turned out to be an **illusion**. He had been dating other women without telling her.

   b. It is only an **illusion** that the sun sets and rises. It is really the earth that is turning away from and then towards the sun.

5 **impact**
(im'-pakt)
-*noun*

   a. When birds accidentally fly into windows, the **impact** often kills them.

   b. That boxer punches with such force that the **impact** of his uppercut can knock out most opponents.

6 **imply**
(im-plī')
-*verb*

   a. To Sherlock Holmes, the clues **implied** that the murderer was an elderly man who carried a cane.

   b. When my friend asked me, "Do you feel all right?" she **implied** that I did not look well.

7 **novice**
(nov'-is)
-*noun*

   a. Since Roger has never played tennis, he will have to join the class for **novices**.

   b. "Don't buy an expensive camera for a **novice**," said the saleswoman. "Let your son first get some experience with a cheap camera."

8 **obstacle**
(ob'-stə-kəl)
-*noun*

   a. I'd better clean my apartment soon. There are too many **obstacles** on the floor between my bed and the refrigerator.

   b. The major **obstacle** to Hal's getting a promotion is his laziness.

Matching Words and Definitions

Check your understanding of the eight words by matching each word with its definition. Look back at the sentences in "Eight Words in Context" as needed to decide on the meaning of each word.

_e_ 1. **endorse**

_c_ 2. **hypocrite**

_h_ 3. **idealistic**

_d_ 4. **illusion**

_g_ 5. **impact**

_a_ 6. **imply**

_f_ 7. **novice**

_b_ 8. **obstacle**

a. to express indirectly; suggest

b. a barrier; something that interferes

c. one who claims to be something he or she is not; an insincere person

d. a mistaken view of reality; an image leading to a false impression

e. to support; express approval of; to state in an ad that one supports a product or service, usually for a fee

f. a beginner; someone new to a field or activity

g. the force of one thing striking another

h. characterized by an emphasis on ideals and principles over practical considerations

CAUTION: Do not go any further until you are sure the above answers are correct. If you have studied the "Eight Words in Context," you will know how to match each word. Then you can use the matches to help you in the following practices. Your goal is to reach a point where you don't need to check definitions at all.

➤Sentence Check 1

Complete each sentence below with the most suitable word from the box. Use each word once.

endorse	hypocrite	idealistic	illusion
impact	imply	novice	obstacle

1. Poems often _____ an idea. That is, they hint at the idea rather than state it directly.

2. I was such a(n) _____ at computers that I didn't even know how to insert a disk.

3. Karen is the least _____ person I know. She is guided only by a desire to get ahead.

4. Don't be such a(n) _____! If you don't like Arlene, then you shouldn't pretend that you do.

5. An actress hired to _____ meat products on TV was fired when it was learned she rarely ate meat herself.

6. Ballet dancers sometimes break their toes when they land with too great a(n) _____ after a leap.

7. I can never drive straight into our driveway because there are always _____s there — tricycles, garbage cans, or toys.

8. When the moon is low in the sky, it looks much larger than when it appears overhead. This difference in size, however, is only a(n) _____.

Now check your answers to these questions by turning to page 117. Going over the answers carefully will help you prepare for the next two checks, for which answers are not given.

➤ Sentence Check 2

Complete each sentence below with two words from the following list. Use each word once.

endorse	hypocrite	idealistic	illusion
impact	imply	novice	obstacle

1-2. "Just because I let them meet in the church basement," said Reverend Lucas, "does not

_____ that I _____ everything the group stands for."

3-4. When the first soldier to fly in an airplane took off in 1908, he had no _____ about

the danger, but he never expected to die from the _____ of crashing into a cemetery wall.

5-6. The first Peace Corps volunteers may have been _____, but they were tough about

their dreams. No _____ would keep them from working for a better world.

7-8. Because she was just out of college, Faye was a(n) _____ at interviewing job

applicants. Nevertheless, she could see that Perry was a(n) _____ who boasted about job skills he didn't have.

➤ Final Check: Night Nurse

Here is a final opportunity for you to strengthen your knowledge of the eight words. First read the following passage carefully. Then fill in each blank with a word from the box at the top of this page. (Context clues will help you figure out which word goes in which blank.) Use each word once.

I'm no (1)_____, so I'll admit I sometimes wish I'd never taken the job of nurse

on the midnight shift. No one in my family would (2)_____ my decision, and

maybe they were right. I had no (3)_____ about the difficulty of the work. I knew

the emergency room would be tough, but I wasn't going to let that be an (4)_____.

Still, as a (5) _____, I guess I did start out more (6)_____ about

helping the world than I am now, ten months later. I don't mean to (7)_____ that

I've soured on nursing, because I haven't. I've just gotten a better idea of what to expect.

The work is at one of the city's biggest hospitals. More often than not, each shift brings a series of

blood-drenched cases. There are shootings and stabbings, and I often see skull fractures showing the

(8)_____ of baseball bats on human heads.

The other day, when I went to buy some shoes for work, the clerk asked me, "What kind of soles

would you like?"

Before I could stop myself, I answered, "Some that won't slip in blood."

SCORES: Sentence Check 2 _____ %   **Final Check** _____ %
Enter your scores above and in the vocabulary performance chart on the inside back cover of the book.

Number right: 8 = 100%   7 = 88%   6 = 75%   5 = 63%   4 = 50%   3 = 38%   2 = 25%   1 = 13%

Previewing the Words

Find out how many of the eight words in this chapter you already know. Try to complete each sentence with the most suitable word from the list below. Use each word once.

Leave a sentence blank rather than guessing at an answer. Your purpose here is just to get a sense of the eight words and what you may know about them.

concede	conservative	denounce	deter
scapegoat	superficial	sustain	transition

1. Under oath in court, the senator was finally willing to _____ that he had taken bribes.

2. When Dad was furious about the holes in the garden, I was afraid to confess I had been digging for buried treasure. So I blamed my dog Speck for the mess, making him the _____.

3. Making the _____ from a small junior high school to a large high school can be very difficult for shy students.

4. The conversation at the party was _____. No one said anything deeper than "Boy, it's cold outside."

5. Jesse is very _____ in his eating habits. He eats only meat and potatoes, refusing to try anything new.

6. Although the runner was still moving fast, he couldn't _____ the speed at which he had begun the race.

7. Throughout the heated campaign, the two political candidates continued to _____ each other as ineffective and dishonest.

8. The fact that only one person in ten is accepted into that nursing program didn't _____ Elena from applying.

Now check your answers by turning to page 117. Fix any mistakes and fill in any blank space by writing in correct answers. By doing so, you will complete this introduction to the eight words.

You're now ready to strengthen your knowledge of the words you already know and to master the words you're only half sure of, or don't know at all. Turn to the next page.

Eight Words in Context

Figure out the meanings of the following eight words by looking *closely and carefully* at the context in which the words appear. Doing so will prepare you for the matching test and the practices on the two pages that follow.

1 **concede**
(kən-sēd')
-*verb*

   a. Our aunt hates to admit an error. She will never **concede** that she might be wrong.

   b. After pretending it was easy learning to use the new computer, Ross had to **concede** he was struggling and ask for help.

2 **conservative**
(kən-sûr'-və-tiv)
-*adjective*

   a. My **conservative** relatives were shocked when I broke with tradition and wore a rose-colored wedding gown.

   b. When the mayor suggested a new method of recycling garbage, a **conservative** member of the audience called out, "What we've done in the past is good enough. Why change things?"

3 **denounce**
(di-nouns')
-*verb*

   a. During the Nazi rule, anyone in Germany who publicly **denounced** Hitler—as cruel or mad—risked imprisonment, torture, and death.

   b. When Eugene said he saw me steal from another student's locker, I **denounced** him as a liar.

4 **deter**
(di-tûr')
-*verb*

   a. No one is sure how much the threat of execution **deters** murder.

   b. Beth's parents disapproved of her dating someone from a different culture, but their prejudice didn't **deter** her—she still dated Po-Yen.

5 **scapegoat**
(skāp'-gōt')
-*noun*

   a. Several girls put dye into their high school swimming pool. In need of a **scapegoat**, they then blamed another student who knew nothing about the prank.

   b. Because the manager wanted a **scapegoat** for his own mistake, he fired an innocent employee.

6 **superficial**
(soo'-pər-fish'-əl)
-*adjective*

   a. Sal and Anita are interested only in appearances. They are so **superficial** that it's impossible to have a deep friendship with them.

   b. My teacher said my essay on divorce was too **superficial**, that I didn't go into the subject with enough depth.

7 **sustain**
(sə-stān')
-*verb*

   a. My diets usually last three days at the most. I can't **sustain** my willpower any longer than that.

   b. The singer can **sustain** a high note for almost a minute.

8 **transition**
(tran-zish'-ən)
-*noun*

   a. Mark's parents were amazed at how easily he made the **transition** from full-time student to full-time employee.

   b. "The **transition** from being childless to being a parent is drastic," said the new father. "Last week, only two quiet people lived at home. Suddenly, we have a third, noisy resident."

Matching Words and Definitions

Check your understanding of the eight words by matching each word with its definition. Look back at the sentences in "Eight Words in Context" as needed to decide on the meaning of each word.

_____ 1. **concede**

_____ 2. **conservative**

_____ 3. **denounce**

_____ 4. **deter**

_____ 5. **scapegoat**

_____ 6. **superficial**

_____ 7. **sustain**

_____ 8. **transition**

a. lacking depth or meaning; insignificant

b. a change from one activity, condition, or location to another

c. someone blamed for the mistakes of others

d. to admit to something

e. to prevent or discourage

f. to openly condemn; express disapproval of

g. to keep something going; continue

h. tending to resist change; favoring traditional values and views

CAUTION: Do not go any further until you are sure the above answers are correct. If you have studied the "Eight Words in Context," you will know how to match each word. Then you can use the matches to help you in the following practices. Your goal is to reach a point where you don't need to check definitions at all.

➤Sentence Check 1

Complete each sentence below with the most suitable word from the box. Use each word once.

concede	conservative	denounce	deter
scapegoat	superficial	sustain	transition

1. The teenagers who smashed the window made an innocent bystander a _____, claiming he had thrown the rock.

2. To _____ a high grade point average throughout college requires much studying.

3. We turned on the TV and heard a speaker _____ all nuclear arms as "suicidal."

4. Even after Stuart listed scientific facts that support his theory, the teacher refused to _____ Stuart might be right.

5. A childhood stutter didn't _____ Leon. He overcame his speech handicap and reached his goal of being a radio announcer.

6. I try to judge people by their character, not by something as _____ as physical appearance.

7. The _____ from her own apartment to a nursing home has been difficult for my grandmother.

8. When Dawn brought home a boyfriend with purple hair and an earring, her _____ parents—who prefer everything old-fashioned and traditional—nearly fainted.

Now check your answers to these questions by turning to page 117. Going over the answers carefully will help you prepare for the next two checks, for which answers are not given.

➤ *Sentence Check 2*

Complete each sentence below with two words from the following list. Use each word once.

concede	conservative	denounce	deter
scapegoat	superficial	sustain	transition

1-2. Starting with the _____ from home to college, some students neglect high school friendships which they had vowed always to _____.

3-4. If Stan were not so _____, Ellen's lack of money wouldn't _____ him from becoming her friend.

5-6. Mary Ann's parents always _____ her, although she is rarely at fault. She has become the _____ for the entire family.

7-8. Mayor Jones was _____—he preferred traditional solutions. So it was hard for him to _____ that some of the broad-minded ideas of his opponent might work.

➤ *Final Check:* Relating to Parents

Here is a final opportunity for you to strengthen your knowledge of the eight words. First read the following passage carefully. Then fill in each blank with a word from the box at the top of this page. (Context clues will help you figure out which word goes in which blank.) Use each word once.

When I was a kid, my parents were everything to me—the smartest, most interesting, most loving people in the world. But when I turned 13, they seemed suddenly changed. Now they were mean and strict, and so (1)_____ that they disliked every new thing that entered my life. They hated my hair, my music, my friends. Sometimes it seemed they even hated me.

Now that I'm making the (2)_____ from my teen years to adulthood, I have to (3)_____ that my parents aren't so bad. Perhaps, at times, I even made them (4)_____s for problems I had caused myself. Now I'd like to have really deep talks with them, not just the (5)_____ chats we've had lately. But it's hard for us to (6)_____ a conversation about anything but unimportant subjects. Instead, I'd like to tell them my plans and dreams, but I'm afraid they'll (7)_____ my ideas as foolish or wrong. It's hard not to let my fears (8)_____ me from seeking a better relationship with my parents, but I think it's worth a try.

SCORES: Sentence Check 2 _____ %   **Final Check** _____ %
Enter your scores above and in the vocabulary performance chart on the inside back cover of the book.

Number right: 8 = 100%   7 = 88%   6 = 75%   5 = 63%   4 = 50%   3 = 38%   2 = 25%   1 = 13%

UNIT ONE: Test 1

PART A
Choose the word that best completes each sentence and write it in the space provided.

1. **fortify**
   undermine
   compel
   illuminate

   Smoking and drinking _____ your health.

2. **conservative**
   extensive
   impartial
   concise

   Damage to the old car was so _____ that repairs would have

   cost more than the car did.

3. **drastic**
   erratic
   naive
   concise

   The other speaker rambled on for an hour, but Greg was _____.

   Ten minutes and he was done.

4. **comply**
   undermine
   endorse
   isolate

   The nurses asked our union to _____ their strike by signing

   a letter of support.

5. **alternative**
   scapegoat
   impact
   morale

   After I failed my first two algebra quizzes, I decided that the sensible

   _____ to flunking was to get some tutoring.

6. **hypocrite**
   novice
   menace
   refuge

   When Jimmy practiced saying dirty words in first grade, he was only a

   _____ , but by sixth grade he was an expert.

7. **erratic**
   idealistic
   candid
   urban

   One advantage of _____ living is the city's wealth of live

   entertainment, including plays and concerts.

8. **drastic**
   radical
   candid
   lenient

   When my boyfriend agreed with me that my new perm looked terrible, I

   regretted that he's always so _____.

9. **obstacle**
   illusion
   transition
   morale

   At Gene's ten-year high school reunion, he was struck by how many of his

   classmates seemed to have already made the _____ to a
   middle-aged lifestyle.

10. **sustain**
    denounce
    imply
    reminisce

    The soprano was famous for her ability to _____ even the

    highest notes for so long it thrilled her audiences.

(Continues on next page)

PART B
Circle **C** if the italicized word is used **correctly**. Circle **I** if the word is used **incorrectly**.

C   I   11.   Alaskan wolves are definitely a *menace* to humans—they don't attack people.

C   I   12.   The newly fallen snow was so bright under the moonlight that it *illuminated* the entire street.

C   I   13.   In 17th-century Massachusetts, one *lenient* jury hanged a dog accused of being a witch.

C   I   14.   *Impartial* employers often pre-judge overweight job applicants as likely to be lazy.

C   I   15.   Since he wanted to borrow the car that night, Harry decided to *comply* with his mother's request to clean his room.

C   I   16.   The *impact* of the baseball I caught was so great that my hand stung even though I was wearing a mitt.

C   I   17.   New York City's Wall Street is named for a wall built to be an *obstacle* to Indians who might want to enter what was then a small city.

C   I   18.   To some extent, stars are an *illusion*. Because starlight takes thousands of years to reach us, many of the stars we see no longer exist.

C   I   19.   Goldie will never admit that she's been wrong about anything; she'll *concede* she was right to the bitter end.

C   I   20.   Once he laid his eyes on the mint-condition Corvette, nothing could *deter* Paolo from his goal of owning the car.

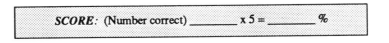

SCORE: (Number correct) _____ x 5 = _____ %

Enter your scores above and in the vocabulary performance chart on the inside back cover of the book.

UNIT ONE: Test 2

PART A
Complete each sentence with a word from the box. Use each word once.

acknowledge	conservative	denounce	drastic	fortify
hypocrite	isolates	morale	refuge	reminisce

1. High stone walls and a ring of water were used to _____ castles against attack.

2. In the 1870's one man took _____ action when his wife refused to serve him breakfast: he divorced her.

3. Americans _____ a great fear of cancer. When surveyed, most report that they fear the disease more than any other.

4. The state park, where no hunting is permitted, serves as a _____ for wildlife that might otherwise be killed.

5. _____ is so low in my office that no one even feels up to discussing how depressed we all are.

6. People who work alone in toll booths must often feel their job _____ them too much, especially late at night.

7. The woman was a _____—she gave speeches about the evils of drugs but was arrested three times for drunk driving.

8. I listened to my grandparents _____ about all the crazy fads they've seen come and go, including T-shirts that gave off a smell of chocolate, garlic, or fish when scratched.

9. Prisoners of war may be tortured until they are willing to publicly _____ their own governments.

10. The Monahans are famous in town for their _____ ways. They have gone to the same church, eaten in the same restaurants and read the same newspaper for three generations.

(Continues on next page)

PART B
Circle **C** if the italicized word is used **correctly.** Circle **I** if the word is used **incorrectly.**

C   I   11.   It is always *appropriate* to yell "Fire!" in a crowded place unless there is really a fire.

C   I   12.   On most American beaches, it's not *legitimate* to go topless.

C   I   13.   Meg is so *idealistic* that the happiest moment of her life is the day her parents bought her a Rolls Royce convertible.

C   I   14.   My little sister is so *naive* about baseball that she knows the names and records of dozens of players.

C   I   15.   Ray is *overt* in his feelings for Julie. He paid for a billboard on Main Street that reads, "Julie, I love you. Ray."

C   I   16.   Why must I always be the family *scapegoat*? Whenever anything goes wrong, I get blamed for it.

C   I   17.   Winston Churchill had such a good memory he could *imply* an entire Shakespearean play word for word.

C   I   18.   Because I've been scatter-brained lately, I decided to *compel* a list of things I needed to do.

C   I   19.   Cesar's moodiness makes his work *erratic*. One week he's a top salesman, and the next week he can't seem to sell a thing.

C   I   20.   Professor Wise gained his *superficial* knowledge on the mating and parenting habits of bedbugs through years of research.

SCORE: (Number correct) _____ x 5 = _____ %

Enter your scores above and in the vocabulary performance chart on the inside back cover of the book.

UNIT ONE: Test 3

PART A: Synonyms
In the space provided, write the letter of the choice that is most nearly the **same** in meaning as the boldfaced word.

_____ 1. **refuge**   **a)** argument   **b)** shelter   **c)** denial   **d)** schedule

_____ 2. **endorse**   **a)** support   **b)** build   **c)** reveal   **d)** think over

_____ 3. **urban**   **a)** mild   **b)** in a city   **c)** noisy   **d)** up-to-date

_____ 4. **alternative**   **a)** lack of interest   **b)** memory   **c)** choice   **d)** insides

_____ 5. **deter**   **a)** encourage   **b)** find   **c)** prevent   **d)** enter

_____ 6. **impact**   **a)** agreement   **b)** force   **c)** danger   **d)** chance

_____ 7. **obstacle**   **a)** vehicle   **b)** aid   **c)** decision   **d)** barrier

_____ 8. **imply**   **a)** obey   **b)** state clearly   **c)** attract   **d)** suggest

_____ 9. **conservative**   **a)** traditional   **b)** cruel   **c)** modern   **d)** to the point

_____ 10. **hypocrite**   **a)** one new to a field   **b)** supporter   **c)** opponent   **d)** insincere person

_____ 11. **reminisce**   **a)** remember   **b)** do again   **c)** look forward to   **d)** overlook

_____ 12. **compel**   **a)** register   **b)** require   **c)** comfort   **d)** allow

_____ 13. **concede**   **a)** admire   **b)** hide   **c)** admit   **d)** strengthen

_____ 14. **drastic**   **a)** extreme   **b)** usual   **c)** rare   **d)** strict

_____ 15. **idealistic**   **a)** young   **b)** seeing the worst   **c)** happy   **d)** emphasizing ideals

_____ 16. **novice**   **a)** fictional character   **b)** beginner   **c)** protector   **d)** one who takes

_____ 17. **scapegoat**   **a)** farmer   **b)** laborer   **c)** planner   **d)** one blamed for others' mistakes

_____ 18. **illusion**   **a)** reality   **b)** false view   **c)** fame   **d)** lighting

_____ 19. **transition**   **a)** change   **b)** hope   **c)** information   **d)** criticism

_____ 20. **morale**   **a)** design   **b)** accident   **c)** spirit   **d)** struggle

(Continues on next page)

PART B: Antonyms
In the space provided, write the letter of the choice that is most nearly the **opposite** in meaning to the boldfaced word.

_____ 21. **naive**   a) experienced   b) having ideals   c) hidden   d) insincere

_____ 22. **comply**   a) enter   b) disobey   c) agree   d) build up

_____ 23. **illuminate**   a) support   b) compete against   c) avoid   d) darken

_____ 24. **menace**   a) female   b) correct view   c) protection   d) harm

_____ 25. **acknowledge**   a) admit   b) convince   c) deny   d) forget

_____ 26. **legitimate**   a) illegal   b) experienced   c) united   d) not chosen

_____ 27. **extensive**   a) praised   b) small   c) improper   d) biased

_____ 28. **lenient**   a) well-known   b) educational   c) deep   d) strict

_____ 29. **candid**   a) dishonest   b) wordy   c) unusual   d) unfriendly

_____ 30. **overt**   a) beginning   b) extreme   c) mild   d) hidden

_____ 31. **denounce**   a) praise   b) weaken   c) compete   d) announce

_____ 32. **sustain**   a) recognize   b) assist   c) discontinue   d) decorate

_____ 33. **impartial**   a) welcome   b) biased   c) elderly   d) strange

_____ 34. **appropriate**   a) famous   b) inconvenient   c) forgotten   d) improper

_____ 35. **undermine**   a) strengthen   b) find   c) describe   d) criticize

_____ 36. **fortify**   a) eat   b) build   c) weaken   d) entertain

_____ 37. **superficial**   a) expensive   b) deep   c) capable   d) legal

_____ 38. **erratic**   a) experienced   b) not required   c) for sale   d) consistent

_____ 39. **concise**   a) short   b) young   c) wordy   d) honest

_____ 40. **isolate**   a) unite   b) state   c) allow   d) interrupt

---

SCORE: (Number correct) _____ x 2.5 = _____ %

Enter your scores above and in the vocabulary performance chart on the inside back cover of the book.

UNIT ONE: *Test 4*

PART A
Complete each sentence in a way that clearly shows you understand the meaning of the boldfaced word. Take a minute to plan your answer before you write.

Example: If you receive a wedding invitation, it is **appropriate** ___*to respond by the date requested.*___

1. One common **transition** that people make in life is _____

   _____

2. Two things that can **illuminate** a room are _____

   _____

3. One way I **compel** myself to study is by _____

   _____

4. One **obstacle** to professional success is _____

   _____

5. A sign of high **morale** on a team is _____

   _____

6. The judge was so **lenient** that _____

   _____

7. Being a **novice** as a waiter, Artie _____

   _____

8. The following remark could **undermine** someone's confidence: _____

   _____

9. I decided to take **drastic** action to improve my social life, so I _____

   _____

10. When I served roast goose and a delicious peanut-butter pie for Thanksgiving dinner, my **conservative**

    brother said, " _____

    _____

(Continues on next page)

PART B

After each boldfaced word are a *synonym* (a word that means the same as the boldfaced word), an *antonym* (a word that means the opposite of the boldfaced word), and a word that is neither. Mark the synonym with an *S* and the antonym with an *A*.

Example: **extensive**	__A__ small	_____ cheap	__S__ large
11-12. **isolate**	_____ include	_____ freeze	_____ separate
13-14. **concise**	_____ old	_____ wordy	_____ brief
15-16. **impartial**	_____ fair	_____ prejudiced	_____ small
17-18. **comply**	_____ understand	_____ obey	_____ disagree
19-20. **urban**	_____ local	_____ city	_____ country

PART C

Use five of the following ten words in sentences. Make it clear that you know the meaning of the word you use. Feel free to use the past tense or plural form of a word.

alternative	candid	deter	erratic	idealistic
illusion	legitimate	menace	superficial	sustain

21. _____

_____

22. _____

_____

23. _____

_____

24. _____

_____

25. _____

SCORE: (Number correct) _____ x 4 = _____ %

Enter your scores above and in the vocabulary performance chart on the inside back cover of the book.

Previewing the Words

Find out how many of the eight words in this chapter you already know. Try to complete each sentence with the most suitable word from the list below. Use each word once.

Leave a sentence blank rather than guessing at an answer. Your purpose here is just to get a sense of the eight words and what you may know about them.

compensate	derive	diversity	moderate
supplement	surpass	tentative	verify

1. Nobody can _____ Meryl Streep in acting ability; she's the best.

2. Make a _____ career choice and then investigate what it involves. If it doesn't interest you, then look for another possible career.

3. The insurance company had to _____ Ernie for the loss of a finger while on a construction job.

4. I _____ satisfaction from keeping my budget down with cheap but delicious foods such as beans and grains.

5. If your pets aren't eating enough, you can _____ their diet with a high-nutrition food.

6. The Sneakers Galore store has sneakers in all price categories: budget, _____ and expensive.

7. Shirley Dowd won the election by only ten votes, so her opponent demanded that the election board

   _____ the results with a recount.

8. Students love the _____ of the menu at the nearby diner. No matter what they feel like eating, they can find it there.

Now check your answers by turning to page 117. Fix any mistakes and fill in any blank spaces by writing in the correct answers. By doing so, you will complete this introduction to the eight words.

You're now ready to strengthen your knowledge of the words you already know and to master the words you're only half sure of, or don't know at all. Turn to the next page.

Eight Words in Context

Figure out the meanings of the following eight words by looking *closely and carefully* at the context in which the words appear. Doing so will prepare you for the matching test and the practices on the two pages that follow.

1 **compensate**
(kom'-pən-sāt')
-*verb*

   a. Some companies still don't **compensate** women for their work as much as they pay men who do the same or similar work.

   b. When an oil rig explosion killed Sam, the company **compensated** his widow with $100,000. However, nothing could really repay her for his loss.

2 **derive**
(di-rīv')
-*verb*

   a. We **derive** plastics from oil. As a result, when oil prices go up, so do the prices of plastic products.

   b. Sarah **derived** pleasure from visiting and reading to old people after school. She enjoyed their company and felt she was doing something worthwhile.

3 **diversity**
(di-vûr'-si-tē)
-*noun*

   a. There's a great **diversity** of breakfast cereals at the supermarket. There are so many different kinds that they take up half an aisle.

   b. "One thing I'm looking for in a college," Sandra told her counselor, "is **diversity**. I want to meet many different kinds of people."

4 **moderate**
(mod'-ər-it)
-*adjective*

   a. The trail was neither flat nor extremely steep—it was **moderate**, for the average hiker.

   b. The prices at this restaurant aren't dirt cheap, but they are **moderate**. So we should be able to have a nice dinner without spending too much.

5 **supplement**
(sup'-lə-mənt)
-*verb*

   a. Many people use vitamins to **supplement** their diet.

   b. At busy times of the year, the department store **supplements** its sales staff with temporary workers.

6 **surpass**
(sər-pas')
-*verb*

   a. You can reach and even **surpass** many of your highest goals.

   b. Denise failed by just inches to **surpass** Rhonda's record leap of five feet in the high jump.

7 **tentative**
(ten'-tə-tiv)
-*adjective*

   a. Our wedding date is **tentative**. We have to be sure Ben's parents are free that weekend before we finalize the date.

   b. Class membership was **tentative** because many students were still dropping and adding courses.

8 **verify**
(ver'-ə-fī')
-*verb*

   a. Race officials **verified** who the winner was by checking a photo of the horses at the finish line.

   b. We'd love to come to the party, but I have to check my calender to **verify** that we're free that evening.

Matching Words and Definitions

Check your understanding of the eight words by matching each word with its definition. Look back at the sentences in "Eight Words in Context" as needed to decide on the meaning of each word.

_____ 1. **compensate**		a. variety
_____ 2. **derive**		b. to make suitable payment to; pay; repay
_____ 3. **diversity**		c. to do better than; go beyond in achievement or quality
_____ 4. **moderate**		d. to test or check the truth or accuracy of something; prove
_____ 5. **supplement**		e. to add to, especially to make up for a lack
_____ 6. **surpass**		f. to receive from a source; get
_____ 7. **tentative**		g. not definite or final
_____ 8. **verify**		h. medium; average; not extreme in quality, degree or amount

CAUTION: Do not go any further until you are sure the above answers are correct. If you have studied the "Eight Words in Context," you will know how to match each word. Then you can use the matches to help you in the following practices. Your goal is to reach a point where you don't need to check definitions at all.

➤ Sentence Check 1

Complete each sentence below with the most suitable word from the box. Use each word once.

compensate	derive	diversity	moderate
supplement	surpass	tentative	verify

1. The Mississippi River _____s its name from Indian words meaning "big river."

2. To _____ that his checkbook balance was correct, Craig added the numbers again.

3. If you aren't very hungry, then take only a _____ helping of food.

4. The exact cast of the movie remains _____ until it is known whether or not Paul Newman is available.

5. Babe Ruth's record number of home runs in a single baseball season was _____(e)d by Roger Maris.

6. The Motor Bureau now _____s the driver's manual with an attached publication on the new driving laws.

7. "Hearing a _____ of opinions is fine," said Lynn. "But it would be nice if everyone in this family could agree once in a while."

8. When my uncle helped me pay for college, he said I could _____ him by helping someone else pay for college when I can afford to.

Now check your answers to these questions by turning to page 117. Going over the answers carefully will help you prepare for the next two checks, for which answers are not given.

➤Sentence Check 2

Complete each sentence below with two words from the following list. Use each word once.

compensate	derive	diversity	moderate
supplement	surpass	tentative	verify

1-2. I have _____ plans to meet Cesar at the Midtown Theatre at eight, but first I must

_____ the show time and call him back.

3-4. By mistake, the textbook left out some important information, so the publishing company decided to

_____ readers—it _____(e)d the text with a free booklet containing
the missing information.

5-6. I _____ great pleasure from having my paintings in an art show, but nothing can

_____ the joy I get in actually doing the painting.

7-8. City College offers a wide _____ of courses and majors at a _____
price. Many students don't realize they have an unusually wide choice of courses at a lower cost than at
many other colleges.

➤Final Check: Job Choices

Here is a final opportunity for you to strengthen your knowledge of the eight words. First read the following
passage carefully. Then fill in each blank with a word from the box at the top of this page. (Context clues will
help you figure out which word goes in which blank.) Use each word once.

After job-hunting for two months, Jessica had to decide whether to work for a fashion magazine or
a clothing store. She already had (1)_____ job offers from both employers. They
would make the offers definite after they were able to (2)_____ the information on
her job application.

In the meanwhile, Jessica thought about the good and bad points of the two jobs. Both offered the
(3)_____ that Jessica liked; she hated doing the same thing every day. Both had
good benefits, such as sick leave and vacation time. However, the two companies would not
(4)_____ her equally. At the clothing store, Jessica would have to start out at a
(5)_____ salary level. With her many expenses, she might even have to find a part-
time job in the evenings to (6)_____ this salary. But there were other, better points.
Working for the store, Jessica would be free to put her many ideas into practice right away. Also, she
would probably move into a better position in about six months. At the fashion magazine, Jessica's
starting salary would far (7)_____ that of the store—she wouldn't have to worry
about money at all. But the possibilities for promotions and raises were not so sure. Jessica could
imagine learning a lot from either job and felt she could (8)_____ much satisfaction
from either one. This would not be an easy decision.

SCORES: Sentence Check 2 _____ %   Final Check _____ %
Enter your scores above and in the vocabulary performance chart on the inside back cover of the book.

Number right: 8 = 100%   7 = 88%   6 = 75%   5 = 63%   4 = 50%   3 = 38%   2 = 25%   1 = 13%

Previewing the Words

Find out how many of the eight words in this chapter you already know. Try to complete each sentence with the most suitable word from the list below. Use each word once.

Leave a sentence blank rather than guessing at an answer. Your purpose here is just to get a sense of the eight words and what you may know about them.

acute	anonymous	apprehensive	arrogant
donor	prominent	prudent	recipient

1. The supermarket puts sale items in _____ places so they can be easily seen.

2. It is more _____ to carry traveler's checks than to carry a large amount of cash.

3. A rich _____ gave the statue of the famous artist to the city, to place in a park.

4. Kim's embarrassment at being overdressed was so _____ that she left the party soon after arriving.

5. As the _____ of a full scholarship, Bernard didn't even have to pay for his college texts.

6. Many folk songs are _____, their composers' names having been lost long before the songs were ever published.

7. After winning his company's Salesman of the Year award twice, Vinnie became overconfident and

   _____ among the other salespeople.

8. The frightened puppy huddled in the corner of the shelter cage. But Margo felt sure he would

   become less _____ after she took him home and he got used to her.

Now check your answers by turning to page 117. Fix any mistakes and fill in any blank spaces by writing in the correct answers. By doing so, you will complete this introduction to the eight words.

You're now ready to strengthen your knowledge of the words you already know and to master the words you're only half sure of, or don't know at all. Turn to the next page.

Eight Words in Context

Figure out the meanings of the following eight words by looking *closely and carefully* at the context in which the words appear. Doing so will prepare you for the matching test and the practices on the two pages that follow.

1 **acute**
(ə-kyo͞ot')
-*adjective*

  a. Gil joked, "This painting looks like something my two-year-old son would do." Then he felt **acute** regret when he learned the artist was standing behind him.

  b. My headache pains were so **acute** that they felt like needles in my head.

2 **anonymous**
(ə-non'-ə-məs)
-*adjective*

  a. Many **anonymous** works are very famous. For example, the author of the well-known Christmas carol "God Rest Ye, Merry Gentlemen" is unknown.

  b. Laura tore up an **anonymous** note saying her husband was seeing another woman. "If the writer was too ashamed to sign the note," said Laura, "why should I believe it?"

3 **apprehensive**
(ap'-ri-hen'-siv)
-*adjective*

  a. Ginny was **apprehensive** as she approached the cow, not knowing if it would try to bite or kick her.

  b. It is natural to be **apprehensive** when making a major purchase such as a computer or a car. Only the very wealthy can afford not to be at all nervous at such times.

4 **arrogant**
(ar'-ə-gənt)
-*adjective*

  a. Having been a very spoiled child, Becky turned out to be a very **arrogant** grownup.

  b. One of the most **arrogant** people I know paid the state extra money to get a custom license plate that reads: "IMBEST."

5 **donor**
(dō'-nər)
-*noun*

  a. Every **donor** to the fund for a new children's hospital will be listed in one of the fund-raising bulletins.

  b. The man's twin sister was the **donor** of his new kidney.

6 **prominent**
(prom'-ə-nənt)
-*adjective*

  a. Crystal's long black hair is so **prominent** that it's the first thing you notice about her.

  b. The most **prominent** balloon in the parade was of Big Bird because it was so large and such a bright yellow.

7 **prudent**
(pro͞od'-ənt)
-*adjective*

  a. Sidney has learned the hard way that it's not **prudent** to tease our ill-tempered dog.

  b. **Prudent** as always, Meg thought carefully before finally deciding which of the used cars would be the best buy.

8 **recipient**
(ri-sip'-ē-ənt)
-*noun*

  a. Katherine Hepburn was the **recipient** of an Academy Award for her role in *On Golden Pond* in 1981, almost fifty years after her first Academy Award.

  b. Doug was the annoyed **recipient** of fourteen pieces of junk mail on the same day.

Matching Words and Definitions

Check your understanding of the eight words by matching each word with its definition. Look back at the sentences in "Eight Words in Context" as needed to decide on the meaning of each word.

_____ 1. **acute**   a. a person who gives, contributes, or donates

_____ 2. **anonymous**   b. frightened; uneasy; anxious

_____ 3. **apprehensive**   c. cautious; careful; wise

_____ 4. **arrogant**   d. severe; sharp

_____ 5. **donor**   e. filled with self-importance; overly proud and vain

_____ 6. **prominent**   f. very noticeable; obvious

_____ 7. **prudent**   g. a person who receives

_____ 8. **recipient**   h. written or given by an unknown or unidentified person

CAUTION: Do not go any further until you are sure the above answers are correct. If you have studied the "Eight Words in Context," you will know how to match each word. Then you can use the matches to help you in the following practices. Your goal is to reach a point where you don't need to check definitions at all.

➤ Sentence Check 1

Complete each sentence below with the most suitable word from the box. Use each word once.

acute	anonymous	apprehensive	arrogant
donor	prominent	prudent	recipient

1. The unsigned letter to the editor was not published because it was the newspaper's policy never to print _____ letters.

2. A final exam causes Phil such _____ anxiety that he has trouble falling asleep the night before taking one.

3. The rich and powerful are sometimes _____—they can mistake always getting their own way for always being right.

4. Carla was so popular that each year she was the _____ of dozens of Valentines.

5. "Your decision to wait to marry until after graduation seems _____ to me," Larry's father said, pleased his son was acting so wisely.

6. Cliff became more and more _____ about the driving test for his license. He was afraid he'd forget to signal, fail to park correctly, or even get into an accident.

7. Because the new tax laws limit certain deductions, there are fewer _____s of art to museums.

8. The bank robber purposely moved with a(n) _____ limp so that witnesses would be sure to notice his "handicap" and put police on someone else's trail.

Now check your answers to these questions by turning to page 117. Going over the answers carefully will help you prepare for the next two checks, for which answers are not given.

➤ *Sentence Check 2*

Complete each sentence below with two words from the following list. Use each word once.

acute	anonymous	apprehensive	arrogant
donor	prominent	prudent	recipient

1-2. The millionaire was so _____ that he refused to be a major _____
to the new town library unless it was named for him.

3-4. It's _____ to keep medication on hand if anyone in the family is subject to

_____ asthma attacks.

5-6. When Joey is very _____, such as when he has to give a speech in class, his stutter

becomes especially _____.

7-8. The famous actress was sometimes the _____ of _____ letters from
fans too shy to sign their names.

➤ *Final Check:* Museum Pet

Here is a final opportunity for you to strengthen your knowledge of the eight words. First read the following
passage carefully. Then fill in each blank with a word from the box at the top of this page. (Context clues will
help you figure out which word goes in which blank.) Use each word once.

"I've got great news!" the museum director shouted to his staff. "Someone wants to give the
museum five million dollars. I don't know who he is—he said that he wishes his gift to remain
(1)_____. There's just one catch," he added.

The employees' smiles faded, and they began to look (2)_____.

"It seems our mystery (3)_____ has a strange fear: he's terribly afraid of cats."

Everyone turned to look at Willard, who had been the museum pet for five years. As usual, the big
orange cat was stretched out in a (4)_____ spot near the entrance. He continued
licking himself, not aware that he was the (5)_____ of everyone's attention.

"I'm afraid Willard will have to go," the director said sadly. "This contributor isn't just a little
afraid of cats; his fear is really (6)_____. Apparently, he panicked when he saw
Willard the last time he came. We can't risk frightening him again. It just wouldn't be
(7)_____—remember, he might give us more money in the future."

"I think it's pretty (8)_____ of this contributor, whoever he is, to ask us to give
up poor old Willard for him, even if he does want to give us the money," one employee said angrily.

"I know you'll miss Willard," the director said, "but I'll be glad to have him come live at my
house. You can all visit him whenever you like." And so Willard found a new home, where he still
lives happily. The museum used the five million dollars to build a new addition, which was known as
the Willard Wing.

SCORES: Sentence Check 2 _____ %   **Final Check** _____ %
Enter your scores above and in the vocabulary performance chart on the inside back cover of the book.

Number right: 8 = 100%   7 = 88%   6 = 75%   5 = 63%   4 = 50%   3 = 38%   2 = 25%   1 = 13%

Previewing the Words

Find out how many of the eight words in this chapter you already know. Try to complete each sentence with the most suitable word from the list below. Use each word once.

Leave a sentence blank rather than guessing at an answer. Your purpose here is just to get a sense of the eight words and what you may know about them.

accessible	awe	cite	exempt
prevail	rational	retort	retrieve

1. Will's reason for running away wasn't _____rational_____—it made no sense at all.

2. Ramps make buildings more _____accessible_____ to people in wheelchairs.

3. When I go bowling with Joan, she usually wins, but I always _____prevail_____ in Scrabble.

4. Before Mitch could _____retrieve_____ the papers he had dropped, the wind scattered them all over the street.

5. Darlene stood in line to get the autograph of her rock-star idol, but when her turn arrived she was too filled with _____awe_____ to speak.

6. No one with a steady job is _____exempt_____ from paying income taxes, although many wish they were.

7. Lisa was sent to the principal's office because of her sarcastic _____retort_____ to the teacher's question.

8. In her speech calling for better protection of children, the mayor will _____cite_____ examples of child abuse.

Now check your answers by turning to page 118. Fix any mistakes and fill in any blank spaces by writing in the correct answers. By doing so, you will complete this introduction to the eight words.

You're now ready to strengthen your knowledge of the words you already know and to master the words you're only half sure of, or don't know at all. Turn to the next page.

Eight Words in Context

Figure out the meanings of the following eight words by looking *closely and carefully* at the context in which the words appear. Doing so will prepare you for the matching test and the practices on the two pages that follow.

1 **accessible**
(ak-ses'-ə-bəl)
-adjective

    a. The department store was not **accessible** from her side of the road, so Kristin looked ahead for a U-turn.

    b. We always hung the candy canes on the Christmas tree's highest branches, where they weren't **accessible** to the younger children.

2 **awe**
(ô)
-noun

    a. Sid is in **awe** of his gymnastics coach, whom he considers the greatest man he knows.

    b. Donna and Frank have different types of idols. While Donna admires Barbara Bush, Frank feels great **awe** for Bruce Springsteen.

3 **cite**
(sīt)
-verb

    a. Jeff was embarrassed but pleased when the teacher **cited** his essay as an example of good writing.

    b. Tired of picking up after her sister, Janet **cited** examples of her sloppiness: "stacks of papers, piles of dirty clothes, and unwashed dishes."

4 **exempt**
(ig-zempt')
-adjective

    a. Since he had never been spanked, my brother thought he was **exempt** from punishment — until he wrote on the walls in ink.

    b. Students with A averages were **exempt** from final exams, so the top three students went to the shore while the rest of us sweated it out on exam day.

5 **prevail**
(pri-vāl')
-verb

    a. Most Hollywood movies have a happy ending: good **prevails** over evil.

    b. Although Kennedy **prevailed** over Nixon in 1960, eight years later Nixon won the presidency.

6 **rational**
(rash'-ə-nəl)
-adjective

    a. Mr. Tibbs isn't **rational**; in addition to believing he came from another planet, he does crazy things like shoveling snow in his pajamas.

    b. The belief that breaking a mirror brings seven years of bad luck isn't **rational**. The only bad luck it could really bring is that of stepping on a sharp piece of broken mirror.

7 **retort**
(ri-tort')
-noun

    a. Sue, who is slender, boasted, "Thin is in." So Pat, who is heavy, gave this **retort**: "Well, fat is where it's at."

    b. When Shelley's balding boyfriend made fun of her new perm, her **retort** was "Jealous?"

8 **retrieve**
(ri-trēv')
-verb

    a. My dog Floyd refuses to **retrieve** a thrown Frisbee. Instead of running to bring it back, he only tilts his head and gives me a questioning look.

    b. I can't **retrieve** my sweater from the library until tomorrow, since the library was closed by the time I realized the sweater was missing.

Matching Words and Definitions

Check your understanding of the eight words by matching each word with its definition. Look back at the sentences in "Eight Words in Context" as needed to decide on the meaning of each word.

_____ 1. **accessible**   a. reasonable; logical

_____ 2. **awe**   b. to mention in support of a point

_____ 3. **cite**   c. a sharp or clever reply

_____ 4. **exempt**   d. easily reached or entered

_____ 5. **prevail**   e. to get (something) back

_____ 6. **rational**   f. to win out; triumph

_____ 7. **retort**   g. a great respect with a touch of fear

_____ 8. **retrieve**   h. free from some unpleasant duty or situation

CAUTION: Do not go any further until you are sure the above answers are correct. If you have studied the "Eight Words in Context," you will know how to match each word. Then you can use the matches to help you in the following practices. Your goal is to reach a point where you don't need to check definitions at all.

➤ *Sentence Check 1*

Complete each sentence below with the most suitable word from the box. Use each word once.

accessible	awe	cite	exempt
prevail	rational	retort	retrieve

1. At the beginning of World War II, Hitler expected his military forces to _prevail_ over all others.

2. I ran back to the ladies' room to _retrieve_ my purse, but someone had already taken it.

3. My brother was _exempt_ from the draft because his vision is so poor.

4. The general's uniform and medals filled Scott with _awe_, but Marla felt the general didn't deserve such respect.

5. The cabinet above the refrigerator was _accessible_ to Janet but not to her roommate Mieko, who was much shorter.

6. When Bridget writes up her experiment, she will _cite_ similar studies by other researchers, to show that her results match theirs.

7. Some people don't think in a(n) _rational_ way. Their thoughts are governed by emotion, not reason.

8. There are at least two versions of the joke in which a customer complains a fly is in his soup. The waiter's _retort_ is either "That's okay—there's no extra charge" or "Don't worry—he won't drink much."

Now check your answers to these questions by turning to page 118. Going over the answers carefully will help you prepare for the next two checks, for which answers are not given.

➤ Sentence Check 2

Complete each sentence below with two words from the following list. Use each word once.

accessible	awe	cite	exempt
prevail	rational	retort	retrieve

1-2. Tony was in _____ of his athletic friend Ben, who seemed to

_____ in any contest of strength or speed.

3-4. The speaker told his high school audience, "I can _____ dozens of adults who thought

they were _____ from the harm of cocaine and eventually lost their jobs and their families."

5-6. It's only _____ that you ask Paul to return your sweater before you sneak into

his room to _____ it behind his back.

7-8. When I complained to the landlord that the kitchen shelves were so high they were

_____ only by ladder, his _____ was, "So get a ladder!"

➤ Final Check: My Headstrong Baby

Here is a final opportunity for you to strengthen your knowledge of the eight words. First read the following passage carefully. Then fill in each blank with a word from the box at the top of this page. (Context clues will help you figure out which word goes in which blank.) Use each word once.

Before my child was born, I truly believed I would be (1)_____ from many of

the restrictions of my friends who were parents. I was sure a baby and a nicely decorated home could

go together. I thought I could just explain to the baby in a calm, (2)_____ manner

that there were certain objects in the house not to be touched. But now I am a mother, and I am in

(3)_____ of a tiny infant's amazing abilities. I've learned that when an adult and a

baby disagree, the baby will almost always (4)_____. I've learned, too, that a child

who can't even crawl can somehow move its little body over to an object that attracts it. It took me a

while to admit defeat—I could (5)_____ examples of vases broken and books

chewed into pulp—but I finally gave up. I look at my formerly attractive house now and see that every

surface (6)_____ to the baby has been cleared of everything but toys. So now, when

my childless friends laugh at me as I (7)_____ my belongings from the uppermost

shelves of the house, this is my (8)_____: "I'll listen to you when you have a kid of

your own."

SCORES: Sentence Check 2 _____ %   Final Check _____ %

Enter your scores above and in the vocabulary performance chart on the inside back cover of the book.

Number right: 8 = 100%   7 = 88%   6 = 75%   5 = 63%   4 = 50%   3 = 38%   2 = 25%   1 = 13%

Previewing the Words

Find out how many of the eight words in this chapter you already know. Try to complete each sentence with the most suitable word from the list below. Use each word once.

Leave a sentence blank rather than guessing at an answer. Your purpose here is just to get a sense of the eight words and what you may know about them.

elapse	evasive	fluent	infer
lethal	obsession	ordeal	persistent

1. His girl friend became such an _____ for my son that he could think of little else.

2. While Maria can hardly speak Spanish, her mother is _____ in it.

3. It is always a great _____ for most people to give a speech in front of a crowd of strangers.

4. Just because a book is long is no reason to _____ it is boring.

5. Several hours would _____ before the emergency-room doctor was able to tell me my father would live.

6. When the police questioned Mr. Shaw, he was _____, giving no specific details that the police could follow up on.

7. Abby was _____ in her efforts to change the Little League's boys-only rule. After seven months of trying, she was finally allowed to join the team.

8. The bite of a black widow spider can be _____, but if treatment is prompt, death can be prevented.

Now check your answers by turning to page 118. Fix any mistakes and fill in any blank spaces by writing in the correct answers. By doing so, you will complete this introduction to the eight words.

You're now ready to strengthen your knowledge of the words you already know and to master the words you're only half sure of, or don't know at all. Turn to the next page.

Eight Words in Context

Figure out the meanings of the following eight words by looking *closely and carefully* at the context in which the words appear. Doing so will prepare you for the matching test and the practices on the two pages that follow.

1 **elapse**
(i-laps')
-verb

   a. When I'm busy with work I enjoy, the hours seem to **elapse** quickly.

   b. Although four years had **elapsed** since I last saw Marian, we talked as if we'd never parted.

2 **evasive**
(i-vā'-siv)
-adjective

   a. The Roberts worried about their son when he became **evasive** about where he had been and what he'd been doing.

   b. We didn't want anyone at school to know our father was in jail, so we were **evasive** about him, saying only, "He has to be away for a while."

3 **fluent**
(floo'-ənt)
-adjective

   a. To work in a foreign country, it helps to be **fluent** in its language.

   b. Jenna wanted to hear what was wrong with her car in simple, everyday words. She was not **fluent** in the language of auto mechanics.

4 **infer**
(in-fûr')
-verb

   a. The fact that the old man left his fortune to strangers led us to **infer** he was not fond of his children.

   b. Since you went hiking on Super Bowl Sunday, I **inferred** you were not a football fan.

5 **lethal**
(lē'-thəl)
-adjective

   a. My father is not alive today because of the **lethal** combination of driving and drinking.

   b. Jake is so good at karate that his hands are **lethal** weapons. Because he realizes he could kill somebody, he wouldn't use karate lightly.

6 **obsession**
(əb-sesh'-ən)
-noun

   a. Psychologists help people troubled by **obsessions** to gain control over their thinking, so they are not bothered by the same thoughts over and over.

   b. Going to the racetrack was at first just a hobby. But the track has become such an **obsession** that I can't seem to stop going there.

7 **ordeal**
(ôr-dēl')
-noun

   a. Even if you are in good physical condition, running cross-country is an **ordeal**.

   b. Hannah came out of the difficult three-hour test, sighed, and said, "What an **ordeal**. I'm worn out."

8 **persistent**
(pər-sis'-tənt)
-adjective

   a. At first Tony wouldn't go out with Lola, but she was **persistent** in asking him. Now they're engaged.

   b. I am a very **persistent** salesman. I work with customers for as long as it takes for them to buy something.

Matching Words and Definitions

Check your understanding of the eight words by matching each word with its definition. Look back at the sentences in "Eight Words in Context" as needed to decide on the meaning of each word.

_____ 1. **elapse**		a. to draw a conclusion from evidence
_____ 2. **evasive**		b. an idea or feeling which someone is overly concerned about
_____ 3. **fluent**		c. a very difficult or painful experience
_____ 4. **infer**		d. deliberately unclear
_____ 5. **lethal**		e. able to cause death; deadly
_____ 6. **obsession**		f. refusing to quit; stubbornly continuing
_____ 7. **ordeal**		g. to pass or slip by (usually said of time)
_____ 8. **persistent**		h. able to speak a language with skill and ease

CAUTION: Do not go any further until you are sure the above answers are correct. If you have studied the "Eight Words in Context," you will know how to match each word. Then you can use the matches to help you in the following practices. Your goal is to reach a point where you don't need to check definitions at all.

➤*Sentence Check 1*

Complete each sentence below with the most suitable word from the box. Use each word once.

elapse	evasive	fluent	infer
lethal	obsession	ordeal	persistent

1. Roger knew a few Chinese phrases, but he was not _____ enough in Chinese to carry on a conversation.

2. When I'm on a diet, eating pizza becomes an _____ for me.

3. Reporters tried to pin the President down on his plans to rescue the hostages, but he always gave a(n) _____ answer.

4. After ten seconds _____, a bell rings, and the game-show host reads the next question.

5. Selling drugs can be a _____ occupation—there is almost one drug-related murder a day in Philadelphia alone.

6 Going to the veterinarian is a real _____ for our dog, who begins to shiver in fear at the sight of the vet's office.

7. Carlos had to work full-time to support his family, but he still earned his college degree by being

_____ in his studies even when he was busy or tired.

8. It was easy for Professor Anderson to _____ that one of the girls had copied the other's paper — both had the same wording in several paragraphs.

Now check your answers to these questions by turning to page 118. Going over the answers carefully will help you prepare for the next two checks, for which answers are not given.

➤ Sentence Check 2

Complete each sentence below with two words from the following list. Use each word once.

elapse	evasive	fluent	infer
lethal	obsession	ordeal	persistent

1-2. Wild mushrooms were an _____ of my aunt, who picked and ate them whenever

    possible. Unfortunately, her abnormal interest proved _____, for she died after a meal
    of poisonous creamed mushrooms on toast.

3-4. "From your _____ answer," said the teacher, "I _____ you haven't
    studied the chapter."

5-6. Five days _____(e)d before the forest fire was put out. It was an especially difficult

    _____ for the firefighters, who had to get by on very little sleep.

7-8. You must be _____ in learning a language if you wish to become

    _____ in it.

➤ Final Check: A Narrow Escape

Here is a final opportunity for you to strengthen your knowledge of the eight words. First read the following
passage carefully. Then fill in each blank with a word from the box at the top of this page. (Context clues will
help you figure out which word goes in which blank.) Use each word once.

    "They're going to kill us or rape us. They're going to kill us or rape us." The thought had become

an (1)_____—I could think of nothing else. When Sharon and I hopped into the

truck to hitch a ride toward Frankfurt, Germany, we were delighted these two Italian truck drivers

were so friendly. Neither of us was (2)_____ in Italian, but we knew a few Italian

words, and they knew a little English. So we could (3)_____ from their words and

motions that they would take us to Frankfurt after they delivered a package. But then they drove

around for a long time and couldn't seem to make their delivery. Hours

(4)_____(e)d, and I became annoyed. The men apologized for the delay and were

(5)_____ in repeating their promise to get us to Frankfurt. But they became more

and more (6)_____ about exactly when this ride would occur. We finally decided to

stay wherever we were for the night, so we asked to be dropped off. Instead, they drove to an empty

warehouse outside of town. The driver took out a long knife and said, "You sleep here." I cried, "Oh,

no, thank you, we'll get out NOW!" and jumped for the door handle. But the men blocked our exit.

That's when I knew they would kill or rape us. The knife was a (7)_____ weapon,

but even without it they could easily kill us. I just sat there shaking and Sharon sobbed and moaned

and cried. Suddenly, one of the men threw up his hands and yelled, "OUT." He didn't have to ask

twice. We flew out of that truck and back to town. We could hardly believe our

(8)_____ was over and that we were around to tell the tale.

> *SCORES:*   Sentence Check 2 _____ %   **Final Check** _____ %
> Enter your scores above and in the vocabulary performance chart on the inside back cover of the book.

Number right: 8 = 100%   7 = 88%   6 = 75%   5 = 63%   4 = 50%   3 = 38%   2 = 25%   1 = 13%

Previewing the Words

Find out how many of the eight words in this chapter you already know. Try to complete each sentence with the most suitable word from the list below. Use each word once.

Leave a sentence blank rather than guessing at an answer. Your purpose here is just to get a sense of the eight words and what you may know about them.

convey	devise	savor	stimulate
subtle	unique	versatile	vivid

1. The actress was so _____ that she could play any kind of role, from a young villain to an elderly saint.

2. My aunt's remarks are often far from _____. Instead of giving a gentle hint, she will blurt out, "Don't be such a fool!"

3. I _____ the smell of coffee almost more than I enjoy its taste.

4. Some of my dreams are in dull shades of grey. Others are in _____ colors.

5. When Edward saw the Grand Canyon, he made no attempt to describe it on a postcard. He felt the grandness of this natural wonder was too amazing to _____ in words.

6. Even if Mr. Pierce sang his lecture while dancing on his desk, he couldn't _____ my interest in geology—to me, the most boring of subjects.

7. The clever biology student was able to _____ a number of experiments to test the effects of different amounts of light on plant growth.

8. This Egyptian bracelet is _____—no other bracelet in the world is made with the same combination of gems and precious metals.

Now check your answers by turning to page 118. Fix any mistakes and fill in any blank spaces by writing in the correct answers. By doing so, you will complete this introduction to the eight words.

You're now ready to strengthen your knowledge of the words you already know and to master the words you're only half sure of, or don't know at all. Turn to the next page.

Eight Words in Context

Figure out the meanings of the following eight words by looking *closely and carefully* at the context in which the words appear. Doing so will prepare you for the matching test and the practices on the two pages that follow.

1 **convey**
(kən-vā')
-verb

    a. Using sign language, chimpanzees can **convey** such ideas as "Candy sweet" and "Gimme hug."

    b. On my parents' twenty-fifth wedding anniversary, I sent a telegram to **convey** my congratulations and love.

2 **devise**
(di-vīz')
-verb

    a. In the 1880's an American woman **devised** a machine that sprayed dinnerware with hot, soapy water—the first automatic dishwasher.

    b. The police had **devised** a plan to catch the thief, but he escaped through the freight elevator.

3 **savor**
(sā'-vər)
-verb

    a. Katie **savored** the candy bar, eating it bit by bit so that the pleasure would last as long as possible.

    b. Given a rare chance to enjoy the beach, I **savored** every moment under the warm sun.

4 **stimulate**
(stim'-yə-lāt')
-verb

    a. The teacher hoped to **stimulate** her students' interest in reading by choosing books that related to their own lives.

    b. When my father grew tomatoes as big as grapefruits, other neighborhood gardeners wanted to know which fertilizer **stimulated** such amazing growth.

5 **subtle**
(sut'-l)
-adjective

    a. Animal actors are trained to respond to human signals too **subtle** to be noticed by the audience.

    b. Although Virginia was born in Alabama, she has lived up North for many years. As a result, her Southern accent is so **subtle** that some of her friends don't even notice it.

6 **unique**
(yōō-nēk')
-adjective

    a. Any musical performance is **unique**—the music will never again be played in exactly the same way.

    b. My talents are **unique** in my family. For example, I'm the only one who can whistle through my nose.

7 **versatile**
(vûr'-sə-təl)
-adjective

    a. My new computer is **versatile**. It can balance my checkbook, do word processing, keep tax records, and play against me in chess.

    b. Edie is the most **versatile** person I know: she paints, sings, does gymnastics, and is a math whiz.

8 **vivid**
(viv'-id)
-adjective

    a. To make the living room bright and dramatic, we decorated it in **vivid** red.

    b. At funerals, most people wear black or dark grey clothing with no touch of **vivid** color.

Matching Words and Definitions

Check your understanding of the eight words by matching each word with its definition. Look back at the sentences in "Eight Words in Context" as needed to decide on the meaning of each word.

_____ 1. **convey**   a. unlike any other

_____ 2. **devise**   b. to invent; think up; create

_____ 3. **savor**   c. bright in color; striking

_____ 4. **stimulate**   d. hardly noticeable; not obvious

_____ 5. **subtle**   e. to communicate; make known

_____ 6. **unique**   f. to cause to become active or grow; arouse

_____ 7. **versatile**   g. to taste or smell with pleasure; enjoy with appreciation

_____ 8. **vivid**   h. able to do many things well

CAUTION: Do not go any further until you are sure the above answers are correct. If you have studied the "Eight Words in Context," you will know how to match each word. Then you can use the matches to help you in the following practices. Your goal is to reach a point where you don't need to check definitions at all.

➤ *Sentence Check 1*

Complete each sentence below with the most suitable word from the box. Use each word once.

convey	devise	savor	stimulate
subtle	unique	versatile	vivid

1. The chimp _____(e)d a way of reaching the banana that hung from the ceiling. She piled one box on top of another and climbed up.

2. Breathing deeply, I _____(e)d my favorite summer smell—freshly-cut grass.

3. Pam's eyes blinked a _____ message that only her husband saw: "I think we should get ready to leave before it gets any later."

4. The painting—with its bright stripes of shocking pink, green, and yellow—was so

   _____ that it glowed even in dim light.

5. I tried to _____ my rabbit's appetite by offering him choice bits of carrots and celery.

6. Dina's body is so expressive that when she dances she seems able to _____ almost any mood with a single movement.

7. The homemade quilt was prized by its owners for its seemingly _____ pattern, unlike any other they had ever seen.

8. From a child's point of view, a simple brown box is very _____—it can be a dollhouse, a bucket, a desk, or even a funny hat.

Now check your answers to these questions by turning to page 118. Going over the answers carefully will help you prepare for the next two checks, for which answers are not given.

➤ *Sentence Check 2*

Complete each sentence below with two words from the following list. Use each word once.

convey	devise	savor	stimulate
subtle	unique	versatile	vivid

1-2. When Jill applies for a job, it will be to her advantage to _____ to interviewers just how

_____ she is. Employers will welcome her many different skills.

3-4. I _____ the time I have alone with my brother, who is unlike anyone else. He has a

_____ way of looking at things.

5-6. I wish someone would_____ a way to _____ my children's appetites so
they will feel hungry for something besides pizza and peanut butter.

7-8. Rosa enjoys wearing _____ colors, like red and purple, while I prefer more

_____ shades, such as pink and baby blue.

➤ *Final Check:* The Power of Advertising

Here is a final opportunity for you to strengthen your knowledge of the eight words. First read the following
passage carefully. Then fill in each blank with a word from the box at the top of this page. (Context clues will
help you figure out which word goes in which blank.) Use each word once.

I am convinced that good advertising agencies could sell people last week's garbage. They make
everything sound good. For example, newspaper ads never sell "brightly colored towels." Instead they
sell "petal-soft bath sheets in a variety of (1)_____ rainbow colors." Perfumes in
ads don't make you "smell good"; they "invite you to please that special man in your life with this
(2)_____ yet unmistakable odor of tea roses." Food ads (3)_____
your appetite by offering "a sauce carefully blended to produce an unforgettable taste that you and
your guests will (4)_____." Clothing ads (5)_____ the idea that
if you wear a particular suit or dress, you will be classier than the next person. Other ads, such as those
for computers, tell you how (6)_____ their products will make you, suggesting that
they will give you more skills than others have. Advertisements must have wide appeal to attract
millions of people. Yet they must also convince all those people that they will be
(7)_____ if they buy a particular product. I bet if an advertising agency wanted to
sell last week's garbage, it would simply (8)_____ an ad saying, "Nowhere else can
you find a gift with so powerful an aroma that it overflows with bittersweet memories of yesterday, yet
hints that it will grow stronger with each passing day."

SCORES: Sentence Check 2 _____ %   **Final Check** _____ %
Enter your scores above and in the vocabulary performance chart on the inside back cover of the book.

Number right: 8 = 100%   7 = 88%   6 = 75%   5 = 63%   4 = 50%   3 = 38%   2 = 25%   1 = 13%

UNIT TWO: *Test 1*

PART A
Choose the word that best completes each sentence and write it in the space provided.

1. **arrogant**
   rational
   moderate
   anonymous

   The editor refuses to print _____ letters. She believes

   people should know whose opinion they are reading.

2. **savor**
   retrieve
   infer
   stimulate

   I used a fishing pole to _____ my hat from the duck pond.

3. **devised**
   retorted
   surpassed
   conveyed

   I knew Jackie would do well in the pole-vault event, but her wonderful perfor-

   mance _____ even my expectations.

4. **subtle**
   prudent
   accessible
   vivid

   Lisa, who is unusually short, had her kitchen built with cabinets low enough to

   be _____ to her.

5. **versatile**
   fluent
   subtle
   lethal

   Separately, the seasonings I put in my pizza sauce are _____.

   Combined, however, they have a strong flavor.

6. **ordeal**
   diversity
   retort
   recipient

   Rita turned her _____ of being lost in the desert into good

   fortune by selling the story to a movie studio.

7. **supplement**
   prevail
   devise
   elapse

   After denting the fender of my parents' car, I let several months

   _____ before I asked to borrow the car again.

8. **surpass**
   savor
   elapse
   convey

   Using only motions, Tina managed to _____ the message to

   Jerry that she would meet him at the Student Center at two o'clock.

9. **cited**
   derived
   verified
   compensated

   We usually don't think about the fact that our books, newspapers, and wooden

   furniture are all _____ from trees.

10. **elapse**
    verify
    stimulate
    derive

    Since kids sometimes call in prank orders to pizza parlors, some pizza clerks

    now call back to _____ that each order is sincere.

(Continues on next page)

PART B
Circle **C** if the italicized word is used **correctly**. Circle **I** if the word is used **incorrectly**.

C   I   11.   During my history teacher's lecture, I was soon able to *infer* her opinion about the U.S. involvement in Vietnam.

C   I   12.   Tony was disappointed when he *prevailed* in the student council election. Maybe he'll do better next year.

C   I   13.   I get tired of Pat's guitar playing. He's so *versatile* that he just plays the same three chords over and over.

C   I   14.   After being the *recipient* of seven speeding tickets in one month, Marylee lost her license.

C   I   15.   Owen bragged that when he hit it rich he was going to buy his mom the most *moderate* diamond necklace in town.

C   I   16.   It's easy to find Dwight's house because of the *prominent* display of pink flamingos on the lawn.

C   I   17.   The high school seniors are *donors* of college scholarships, which they received from a generous local business owner.

C   I   18.   When my sister doubled over with sudden, *acute* pain, we suspected her appendix had become infected.

C   I   19.   Lucy was *apprehensive* about going to an Indian restaurant with Lloyd; she loved spicy Indian food more than anything.

C   I   20.   To make my point that college can be as stressful as a full-time job, I *cited* the pressures of being a student.

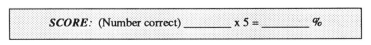

SCORE: (Number correct) _____ x 5 = _____ %

Enter your scores above and in the vocabulary performance chart on the inside back cover of the book

UNIT TWO: Test 2

PART A
Complete each sentence with a word from the box. Use each word once.

awe	compensate	diversity	lethal	prudent
rational	retort	savor	supplement	tentative

1. I hung my dress outside the cleaners when the owner refused to _____ me for ruining it by running the colors together.

2. It's thrilling to watch Michael Jordan play basketball. His athletic ability fills me with

   _____ .

3. After running out of gas on the way to the hospital for an emergency, I decided it was

   _____ to keep the tank full at all times.

4. The victim of the mugger made a _____ identification of her attacker from a photo. But she said she would have to see him in person to be sure.

5. The young mother was still giving her toddler only milk. The doctor explained that it was

   time for her to _____ the child's diet with solid food.

6. I like our women's group because of its _____ . Among the members are grandmothers, young mothers, and young single women as well as black, Hispanic and white women.

7. It's dangerous to mix chlorine bleach and other household cleaners. The combination can

   produce _____ fumes.

8. Knowing the ice cream would be his last before beginning his diet, Jon took time to

   _____ every rich spoonful.

9. Rosa is very _____ about her love life. She lists a guy's good and bad qualities before deciding if she'll date him again.

10. When Paul complained, "Women and computers are both impossible to understand," his wife

    gave this _____: "No, you just don't know how to turn either one on."

(Continues on next page)

PART B
Circle **C** if the italicized word is used **correctly**. Circle **I** if the word is used **incorrectly**.

C   I   11.   Although our teacher is *fluent* in French and Italian, her Russian is shaky.

C   I   12.   At some health clinics, people with little income are *exempt* from all fees.

C   I   13.   After my sister turned down Gabe's first request for a date, he was so *persistent* that he gave up.

C   I   14.   Lynn has repeatedly asked Brian what exactly he does for a living, but she always gets an *evasive* answer like "I'm in sales."

C   I   15.   Phil has such an *obsession* with his looks that he sometimes wears socks that don't match or forgets to comb his hair.

C   I   16.   My brother's basement apartment must be *unique*. It's the only place I've ever seen with a bathtub right in the middle of the kitchen.

C   I   17.   My overactive young nephew takes medicine to *stimulate* his tendency to race around the house and throw things.

C   I   18.   Someone has *devised* sunglasses that serve as "eyes in the back of your head." Put them on and you see what's behind you.

C   I   19.   Sally always dresses in *vivid* colors, such as pastel pink or light grey.

C   I   20.   Every store has its share of *arrogant* customers who push to the front of the line and demand to be waited on out of turn.

SCORE: (Number correct) _____ x 5 = _____ %

Enter your scores above and in the vocabulary performance chart on the inside back cover of the book.

UNIT TWO: Test 3

PART A: Synonyms
In the space provided, write the letter of the choice that is most nearly the **same** in meaning as the boldfaced word.

_____ 1. **compensate**   **a)** pay   **b)** pass   **c)** prove   **d)** decide

_____ 2. **retort**   **a)** add to   **b)** know   **c)** reply   **d)** get back

_____ 3. **awe**   **a)** hate   **b)** respect   **c)** regret   **d)** confusion

_____ 4. **lethal**   **a)** extreme   **b)** modest   **c)** wise   **d)** deadly

_____ 5. **fluent**   **a)** smooth-speaking   **b)** full   **c)** not obvious   **d)** reachable

_____ 6. **savor**   **a)** win   **b)** answer   **c)** enjoy   **d)** hide

_____ 7. **elapse**   **a)** please   **b)** pass   **c)** outdo   **d)** gather

_____ 8. **retrieve**   **a)** send   **b)** walk around   **c)** think up   **d)** get back

_____ 9. **verify**   **a)** prove   **b)** add to   **c)** repay   **d)** contradict

_____ 10. **infer**   **a)** reply   **b)** mention   **c)** conclude   **d)** do better than

_____ 11. **accessible**   **a)** having great variety   **b)** logical   **c)** not obvious   **d)** reachable

_____ 12. **obsession**   **a)** pay   **b)** painful experience   **c)** variety   **d)** idea of extreme concern

_____ 13. **exempt**   **a)** wise   **b)** lively   **c)** excused   **d)** fearful

_____ 14. **surpass**   **a)** support   **b)** outdo   **c)** lose   **d)** invent

_____ 15. **cite**   **a)** mention   **b)** locate   **c)** pass   **d)** delay

_____ 16. **apprehensive**   **a)** unclear   **b)** able to do many things well   **c)** deadly   **d)** fearful

_____ 17. **devise**   **a)** create   **b)** receive   **c)** prevent   **d)** repay

_____ 18. **supplement**   **a)** win out   **b)** owe   **c)** add to   **d)** provide the moving force

_____ 19. **convey**   **a)** invent   **b)** communicate   **c)** cause to grow   **d)** test

_____ 20. **versatile**   **a)** having many skills   **b)** average   **c)** musical   **d)** not final

(Continues on next page)

PART B: Antonyms

In the space provided, write the letter of the choice that is most nearly the **opposite** in meaning to the boldfaced word.

_____ 21. **prevail**   a) discourage   b) give   c) hide   d) lose

_____ 22. **arrogant**   a) modest   b) helpful   c) relaxed   d) stubborn

_____ 23. **rational**   a) illegal   b) unreasonable   c) unreliable   d) mild

_____ 24. **anonymous**   a) unknown   b) common   c) identified   d) dull

_____ 25. **donor**   a) boss   b) organizer   c) newcomer   d) one who receives

_____ 26. **prominent**   a) bright   b) misleading   c) unnoticeable   d) unwise

_____ 27. **diversity**   a) disrespect   b) sameness   c) difficulty   d) question

_____ 28. **prudent**   a) unwise   b) unknown   c) shy   d) straightforward

_____ 29. **moderate**   a) conceited   b) old   c) extreme   d) courageous

_____ 30. **derive**   a) give   b) stand still   c) win   d) discourage

_____ 31. **acute**   a) unreasonable   b) mild   c) obvious   d) definite

_____ 32. **persistent**   a) not well-known   b) dull   c) illogical   d) giving up

_____ 33. **recipient**   a) employee   b) one who gives   c) one who asks   d) owner

_____ 34. **evasive**   a) light   b) common   c) straightforward   d) healthy

_____ 35. **subtle**   a) young   b) humble   c) continuing   d) obvious

_____ 36. **vivid**   a) lively   b) dull   c) late   d) required

_____ 37. **ordeal**   a) pleasant experience   b) sale   c) variety   d) question

_____ 38. **tentative**   a) fearful   b) definite   c) misleading   d) illogical

_____ 39. **stimulate**   a) enjoy   b) hint at   c) discourage   d) disappear

_____ 40. **unique**   a) rare   b) famous   c) common   d) unknown

SCORE: (Number correct) _____ x 2.5 = _____ %

Enter your scores above and in the vocabulary performance chart on the inside back cover of the book.

UNIT TWO: Test 4

PART A

Complete each sentence in a way that clearly shows you understand the meaning of the boldfaced word. Take a minute to plan your answer before you write.

    Example: I wanted to **verify** the program's starting time, so I   *checked the listings in <u>TV Guide</u>.*

1. A **unique** color combination for a car would be _____

   _____

2. My sister is so **versatile** that _____

   _____

3. People who write letters to advice columns like to be **anonymous** because _____

   _____

4. Because of her **obsession** with clothes, Sheila _____

   _____

5. Here's an **evasive** answer to "What did you do over vacation?": " _____

   _____

6. Fran decided to **supplement** her income by _____

   _____

7. Pauline is so **arrogant** that when Greg told her she look pretty, she replied _____

   _____

8. While waiting for my turn for a haircut, I felt **apprehensive** because _____

   _____

9. My friend Ted was very **prudent** about his money. For instance, _____

   _____

10. When Joanne asked her husband why he hadn't washed the dinner dishes, his **retort** was, " _____

   _____

(Continues on next page)

(Continues on next page)

59

PART B

After each boldfaced word are a *synonym* (a word that means the same as the boldfaced word), an *antonym* (a word that means the opposite of the boldfaced word), and a word that is neither. Mark the synonym with an *S* and the antonym with an *A*.

Example: **donor**	__A__ receiver	__S__ giver	_____ planner
11-12. **prevail**	_____ lose	_____ triumph	_____ disguise
13-14. **lethal**	_____ harmless	_____ useful	_____ deadly
15-16. **vivid**	_____ bright	_____ angry	_____ colorless
17-18. **subtle**	_____ slight	_____ attractive	_____ obvious
19-20. **awe**	_____ wisdom	_____ contempt	_____ respect

PART C

Use five of the following ten words in sentences. Make it clear that you know the meaning of the word you use. Feel free to use the past tense or plural form of a word.

accessible	compensate	derive	elapse	infer
ordeal	persistent	prominent	retrieve	savor

21. _____

_____

22. _____

_____

23. _____

_____

24. _____

_____

25. _____

SCORE: (Number correct) _____ x 4 = _____ %

Enter your scores above and in the vocabulary performance chart on the inside back cover of the book.

Previewing the Words

Find out how many of the eight words in this chapter you already know. Try to complete each sentence with the most suitable word from the list below. Use each word once.

Leave a sentence blank rather than guessing at an answer. Your purpose here is just to get a sense of the eight words and what you may know about them.

endeavor	equate	impose	indignant
inevitable	option	passive	patron

1. Don't _____ years of schooling with intelligence; they aren't the same thing.

2. My roommate failed half of his courses because he didn't even _____ to learn the material.

3. "Hank is our best _____," said the owner of the donut shop, pointing to a heavy customer eating from a plateful of donuts.

4. Graduating students have the _____ of either attending graduation or receiving their degrees in the mail.

5. My sister and brother-in-law had dated for so long it seemed _____ they would get married.

6. Eddie allowed me to _____ on him by agreeing to type up my ten-page research paper.

7. When his wife accused him of never helping around the house, Mac was _____. Hadn't he just built a deck off the kitchen?

8. I enjoy listening to the stereo, but I'm not just a _____ music lover. I also like to sing and play piano.

Now check your answers by turning to page 118. Fix any mistakes and fill in any blank spaces by writing in the correct answers. By doing so, you will complete this introduction to the eight words.

You're now ready to strengthen your knowledge of the words you already know and to master the words you're only half sure of, or don't know at all. Turn to the next page.

Eight Words in Context

Figure out the meanings of the following eight words by looking *closely and carefully* at the context in which the words appear. Doing so will prepare you for the matching test and the practices on the two pages that follow.

1 **endeavor**
(en-dev'-ər)
-verb

   a. Becky **endeavored** to raise money for Christmas presents by selling candy and cookies door to door.

   b. You are not likely to achieve a goal you will not even **endeavor** to reach.

2 **equate**
(i-kwāt')
-verb

   a. It would be a mistake to **equate** the two teams just because they both have perfect records. One team has played much stronger opponents.

   b. Don't **equate** all homework with busywork. Homework can increase one's understanding of a subject.

3 **impose**
(im-pōz')
-verb

   a. I'd rather rent a car for the trip than **impose** on my girlfriend by borrowing her car.

   b. Roy is always asking favors, yet no one ever seems to notice how much he **imposes** on them.

4 **indignant**
(in-dig'-nənt)
-adjective

   a. My mother becomes **indignant** when she sees parents treat their children with disrespect.

   b. When she was falsely accused of stealing the gold chain, the student became very **indignant**.

5 **inevitable**
(in-ev'-i-tə-bəl)
-adjective

   a. I am such a chocoholic that if you put a brownie in front of me, it is **inevitable** I will eat it.

   b. We try so many ways of looking and staying young, but aging is **inevitable**.

6 **option**
(op'-shən)
-noun

   a. When the mugger said to me, "Give me your wallet or I'll kill you," I didn't like either **option**.

   b. Harry thinks a multiple-choice test allows him to choose more than one **option**.

7 **passive**
(pas'-iv)
-adjective

   a. Taylor is very **passive**. He waits for things to happen instead of making them happen.

   b. Students learn more when they take part in class discussions, instead of being **passive** listeners.

8 **patron**
(pā'-trən)
-noun

   a. The punk-rock star was one of the beauty shop's best **patrons**. She came in at least once a week to change her hair color.

   b. Many of the diner's **patrons** were stagehands who worked at the theater across the street.

Matching Words and Definitions

Check your understanding of the eight words by matching each word with its definition. Look back at the sentences in "Eight Words in Context" as needed to decide on the meaning of each word.

_____ 1. **endeavor**	a. a choice
_____ 2. **equate**	b. to take advantage of
_____ 3. **impose**	c. not active but acted upon
_____ 4. **indignant**	d. sure to happen; unavoidable
_____ 5. **inevitable**	e. to consider as equal, the same, or closely related
_____ 6. **option**	f. to try; attempt
_____ 7. **passive**	g. angry over some insult or injustice
_____ 8. **patron**	h. a steady customer

CAUTION: Do not go any further until you are sure the above answers are correct. If you have studied the "Eight Words in Context," you will know how to match each word. Then you can use the matches to help you in the following practices. Your goal is to reach a point where you don't need to check definitions at all.

➤Sentence Check 1

Complete each sentence below with the most suitable word from the box. Use each word once.

endeavor	equate	impose	indignant
inevitable	option	passive	patron

1. When rats are crowded, it's _____ they will fight with each other.

2. I have only two _____s on my job: I can do what my boss asks, or I can be fired.

3. In our society, we too often _____ happiness with money.

4. Mort isn't a _____ football fan. He actively participates by jumping out of his seat and yelling until he's hoarse.

5. I was the store's most loyal _____ until new management raised the prices, and then I started shopping elsewhere.

6. "I don't want to _____ on you," Scott said, "but if you're going to the post office, would you get me some stamps?"

7. Thomas was understandably _____ when they fired him without a good reason.

8. Mindy _____(e)d to stop her hiccups by putting a paper bag over her head.

Now check your answers to these questions by turning to page 118. Going over the answers carefully will help you prepare for the next two checks, for which answers are not given.

➤ Sentence Check 2

Complete each sentence below with two words from the following list. Use each word once.

endeavor	equate	impose	indignant
inevitable	option	passive	patron

1-2. _____ that the boys had thrown rocks at the monkeys and yelled at them, the

zookeeper said, "Don't _____ being an animal with having no feelings."

3-4. Rita, a _____ of Angelo's restaurant for several years, has

_____(e)d without success to copy Angelo's delicious spaghetti sauce.

5-6. "If you remain so _____ that you don't object when Jean takes advantage of you,

she'll just _____ on you more and more," my friend warned.

7-8. Since Sam's family is so poor, it seems _____ he'll work full-time as soon as he

finishes high school. He won't have the _____ of going to college.

➤ Final Check: Waiter

Here is a final opportunity for you to strengthen your knowledge of the eight words. First read the following passage carefully. Then fill in each blank with a word from the box at the top of this page. (Context clues will help you figure out which word goes in which blank.) Use each word once.

The loud voice of the young man at the next table startled me. He was (1)_____

about an undeserved scolding the waiter had received. "Why did you just stand there and take all that

abuse from that old lady? You were like a(n) (2)_____ little child."

"I beg your pardon, Sir," the waiter answered. "That woman is a(n) (3)_____ of

this restaurant. I (4)_____ to treat our customers with respect."

"Even those who (5)_____ on you by being so demanding? Even those who

think they're better than you because you're waiting on them?"

"You seem to (6)_____ my polite manner with weakness," the waiter answered.

"I don't like rude customers, but they're part of the territory of a waiter. Standing up publicly to the

woman may seem like a smart move to you, but it would have made two things

(7)_____: an ugly scene and the loss of my job."

"But you have no (8)_____," the customer insisted. "You can't let people step

on you."

"You're giving me just as hard a time as that woman did," the waiter finally stated. "Why should I

submit to your harassment and not hers?"

SCORES: Sentence Check 2 _____ %   **Final Check** _____ %
Enter your scores above and in the vocabulary performance chart on the inside back cover of the book.

Number right: 8 = 100%   7 = 88%   6 = 75%   5 = 63%   4 = 50%   3 = 38%   2 = 25%   1 = 13%

Previewing the Words

Find out how many of the eight words in this chapter you already know. Try to complete each sentence with the most suitable word from the list below. Use each word once.

Leave a sentence blank rather than guessing at an answer. Your purpose here is just to get a sense of the eight words and what you may know about them.

| adapt | dismay | exile | gesture |
| reciprocate | refute | retain | ritual |

1. Plastic storage containers often _____ the odors of foods. I have one that still smells like spaghetti sauce after ten washings.

2. Since Arnie drove me to softball practice last week, I'll _____ and drive him to this week's practice.

3. Although Lena was _____(e)d to learn the application was due in only three days, she decided to try to get it in on time.

4. The tribe performed an ancient dance, a(n) _____ meant to please the gods and bring rain.

5. In a _____ of cooperation, the manager and the head of the union shook hands.

6. I _____(e)d the bill by showing that the cashier had overcharged me for one item.

7. Many Jews were forced to flee Nazi Germany and live in _____, never to return to their native land.

8. When Greg moved from a small Southern town to Boston, he had to _____ to new weather conditions, accents, and customs.

Now check your answers by turning to page 118. Fix any mistakes and fill in any blank spaces by writing in the correct answers. By doing so, you will complete this introduction to the eight words.

You're now ready to strengthen your knowledge of the words you already know and to master the words you're only half sure of, or don't know at all. Turn to the next page.

Eight Words in Context

Figure out the meanings of the following eight words by looking *closely and carefully* at the context in which the words appear. Doing so will prepare you for the matching test and the practices on the two pages that follow.

1 **adapt**
(ə-dapt')
-*verb*

    a. After many years of being only a student, I found it hard to **adapt** to the schedule of a full-time job.

    b. Surprisingly, Gina **adapted** well to California. She thought she would have trouble adjusting to living so far from her family and friends.

2 **dismay**
(dis-mā')
-*verb*

    a. Carmen was **dismayed** when he realized that he wouldn't have enough money to buy a special birthday present for his girlfriend.

    b. The doctor knew it would **dismay** Karl to learn his injured leg would never regain its previous strength.

3 **exile**
(eg'-zīl')
-*noun*

    a. The political rebel decided to end his five-year **exile** and return to his native land to oppose the government.

    b In the movie *The Sound of Music*, the Von Trapp family is forced into **exile** when the Nazis take control of their homeland.

4 **gesture**
(jes'-chər)
-*noun*

    a. As a **gesture** of sympathy, the neighborhood association sent flowers to Milly when her husband died.

    b. The other workers' **gestures** of friendship made Vic feel at home on the first day of his new job.

5 **reciprocate**
(ri-sip'-rə-kāt')
-*verb*

    a. I've done many favors for Anne, but she never **reciprocates** by doing a favor in return.

    b. Alonso treated me to dinner, so I'm going to **reciprocate** by taking him to my favorite restaurant.

6 **refute**
(ri-fyo͞ot')
-*verb*

    a. The lawyer was able to **refute** the defendant's claim that she was home the night of the murder. He had found a witness who saw her in a town bar that night.

    b. Some science-fiction fans were disappointed when photos of Mars **refuted** the idea that intelligent life exists there.

7 **retain**
(ri-tān')
-*verb*

    a. The chairman of the board **retained** control of the firm by firing the president, who opposed him.

    b. "I can usually **retain** my sense of humor," Janice said. "But I lose it totally when I'm laid off and break up with my boyfriend in the same week."

8 **ritual**
(rich'-o͞o-əl)
-*noun*

    a. **Rituals**—set practices that are repeated regularly—are important in most religious traditions.

    b. Each time Mary Ann must fly, she writes a check to a charity, carries it on the plane, and mails it at her destination. She believes this **ritual** guarantees a safe flight.

Matching Words and Definitions

Check your understanding of the eight words by matching each word with its definition. Look back at the sentences in "Eight Words in Context" as needed to decide on the meaning of each word.

_____ 1. **adapt**		a. anything said or done to show one's attitude or intentions
_____ 2. **dismay**		b. to do in return; pay back
_____ 3. **exile**		c. separation from one's native country through force or choice
_____ 4. **gesture**		d. a ceremony; any actions done regularly in a set manner
_____ 5. **reciprocate**		e. to prove wrong or false
_____ 6. **refute**		f. to adjust to a situation
_____ 7. **retain**		g. to keep
_____ 8. **ritual**		h. to discourage; make fearful or uneasy

CAUTION: Do not go any further until you are sure the above answers are correct. If you have studied the "Eight Words in Context," you will know how to match each word. Then you can use the matches to help you in the following practices. Your goal is to reach a point where you don't need to check definitions at all.

➤ Sentence Check 1

Complete each sentence below with the most suitable word from the box. Use each word once.

adapt	dismay	exile	gesture
reciprocate	refute	retain	ritual

1. Getting a D on the first math test of the semester _____(e)d Sean.

2. Antonio tried to _____ my argument, but I was able to prove I was right.

3. As a _____ of support and encouragement, Jeri's friends cheered when it was her turn to bowl in the tournament.

4. To _____ her strength and energy, Mrs. Green does push-ups, sit-ups, and leg-lifts three times a week.

5. As the Ice Age ended, some animals were able to _____ to the new climate. Those who could not adjust failed to survive.

6. The country's new dictator feared having certain political enemies in the country, so he sent them into

   _____.

7. I always send Gordon a birthday card, but he doesn't bother to _____ with a card or phone call on my birthday.

8. Homer always repeats the same baseball _____ before he bats: he twirls his bat three times, stretches his arms, and says, "Okay, okay, this one will be good."

Now check your answers to these questions by turning to page 118. Going over the answers carefully will help you prepare for the next two checks, for which answers are not given.

➤ Sentence Check 2

Complete each sentence below with two words from the following list. Use each word once.

adapt	dismay	exile	gesture
reciprocate	refute	retain	ritual

1-2. "I don't want to _____ you," Jack's lawyer told him, "but it's going to be difficult to _____ the charges against you."

3-4. The Reillys have been so kind to me that I want to _____ in some way. I don't have much money, so I hope they'll understand that a small gift is meant as a _____ of great appreciation.

5-6. Any customary _____, such as the Roman Catholic Mass, helps a church to _____ a sense of tradition.

7-8. The Howards had _____ (e)d well to other cultures, but they were still pleased to retire from the Foreign Service and return to America after their long _____ in Europe and Asia.

➤ Final Check: Adjusting to a New Culture

Here is a final opportunity for you to strengthen your knowledge of the eight words. First read the following passage carefully. Then fill in each blank with a word from the box at the top of this page. (Context clues will help you figure out which word goes in which blank.) Use each word once.

When En-Mei first came to the United States from China, any little problem was enough to (1)_____ her. As a lonely student, she felt as if she had been sent into a forced (2)_____ from her native country. She didn't like American food and tried to limit her diet to Chinese dishes. Otherwise, however, she worked hard to (3)_____ to an unfamiliar country. Soon she overcame her shyness and learned to (4)_____ other students' (5)_____ s of friendship. But En-Mei didn't try to become "all-American"; she wanted to (6)_____ her Chinese identity. She taught her new friends about modern China and tried to (7)_____ mistaken ideas they had about her country. She even found a group of friends willing to learn tai chi, an ancient Chinese exercise (8)_____ that benefits body and spirit. Living in America wasn't always easy. Sometimes En-Mei would miss her family so badly that her former unhappiness would return. But such times were increasingly rare. By the end of her first year here, En-Mei even found she had become a devoted fan of pizza and apple pie.

SCORES: Sentence Check 2 _____ %   Final Check _____ %
Enter your scores above and in the vocabulary performance chart on the inside back cover of the book.

Number right: 8 = 100%   7 = 88%   6 = 75%   5 = 63%   4 = 50%   3 = 38%   2 = 25%   1 = 13%

Previewing the Words

Find out how many of the eight words in this chapter you already know. Try to complete each sentence with the most suitable word from the list below. Use each word once.

    Leave a sentence blank rather than guessing at an answer. Your purpose here is just to get a sense of the eight words and what you may know about them.

elaborate	emerge	exotic	frugal
indifferent	liberal	mediocre	notable

1. Since I'm not earning much money, I try to be _____.

2. The bride planned the wedding in _____ detail, not forgetting the least thing; the groom, however, forgot to come.

3. Usually a C grade indicates neither the best nor the worst job, but work that is average, or

   _____.

4. Looking out over the water, we saw a tiny submarine _____ from below the surface.

5. Tamara is such a talented actress that we all expect her to become a _____ film or TV star.

6. The kiwi fruit, grown in New Zealand, is one of several _____ fruits now commonly sold in supermarkets.

7. I care greatly whether a Democrat or Republican wins the election. But my brother, who has no real

   interest in politics, is _____ about the election.

8. The ice-cream parlor was known for its _____ servings—huge scoops dripping with syrup.

Now check your answers by turning to page 118. Fix any mistakes and fill in any blank spaces by writing in the correct answers. By doing so, you will complete this introduction to the eight words.

    You're now ready to strengthen your knowledge of the words you already know and to master the words you're only half sure of, or don't know at all. Turn to the next page.

Eight Words in Context

Figure out the meanings of the following eight words by looking *closely and carefully* at the context in which the words appear. Doing so will prepare you for the matching test and the practices on the two pages that follow.

1 **elaborate**
(i-lab'-ər-it)
-adjective

  a. The dinner required **elaborate** preparation. Each course included a complicated favorite dish of one of the guests.

  b. Irma's quilt was very **elaborate**. She used tiny stitches to sew on the very detailed pattern.

2 **emerge**
(i-mûrj')
-verb

  a. Anna **emerged** from the dressing room, looking beautiful in a blue prom gown.

  b. When the chick **emerged** from its egg, it was tired and wet, but a day later it was a fluffy yellow ball of energy.

3 **exotic**
(ig-zot'-ik)
-adjective

  a. Orchids are grown in the U.S., not just in foreign countries. So Americans really should not consider the flower **exotic**.

  b. Ross has an **exotic** accent of some kind, but I can't put my finger on just what country he comes from.

4 **frugal**
(froo'-gəl)
-adjective

  a. You can stretch your dollars by being **frugal**. For example, using store coupons and waiting for expensive items to be on sale can save a lot of money.

  b. Diane buys designer jeans, but because I need to be more **frugal**, I buy store-brand jeans.

5 **indifferent**
(in-dif'-ər-ənt)
-adjective

  a. Does our society have no interest in homeless children? Are we **indifferent** to the many families who can no longer afford to pay rent?

  b. Because her husband was **indifferent** to how the apartment would be decorated, Kathy felt free to do the job any way she wanted.

6 **liberal**
(lib'-ər-əl)
-adjective

  a. Martin Lopez has no children, so he gives **liberal** Christmas and birthday gifts to his nephews and nieces.

  b. Norma left the waiter a **liberal** tip because he had been especially friendly and helpful.

7 **mediocre**
(mē-dē-ō'-kər)
-adjective

  a. The mystery movie was neither terrible nor great; it was **mediocre**.

  b. Although Hank can be quite funny, his jokes are only **mediocre** compared to those of the best comedians.

8 **notable**
(nō'-tə-bəl)
-adjective

  a. Winning the Nobel Prize can make a little-known scientist into a **notable** world figure.

  b. Abraham Lincoln's "Gettysburg Address" is surely his most **notable** speech, especially among those many Americans who memorized it in school.

Matching Words and Definitions

Check your understanding of the eight words by matching each word with its definition. Look back at the sentences in "Eight Words in Context" as needed to decide on the meaning of each word.

_____ 1. **elaborate**	a. to rise up or come forth
_____ 2. **emerge**	b. famous; widely known
_____ 3. **exotic**	c. having no real interest; unconcerned
_____ 4. **frugal**	d. generous
_____ 5. **indifferent**	e. done with great attention to details; complex
_____ 6. **liberal**	f. average; ordinary; neither very bad nor very good
_____ 7. **mediocre**	g. foreign; from a different part of the world; strange or different in an appealing way
_____ 8. **notable**	h. thrifty; avoiding unnecessary expenses

CAUTION: Do not go any further until you are sure the above answers are correct. If you have studied the "Eight Words in Context," you will know how to match each word. Then you can use the matches to help you in the following practices. Your goal is to reach a point where you don't need to check definitions at all.

➤ *Sentence Check 1*

Complete each sentence below with the most suitable word from the box. Use each word once.

elaborate	emerge	exotic	frugal
indifferent	liberal	mediocre	notable

1. While my father didn't do badly in school, he wasn't a great student. So he's proof it's possible to have a

   successful career despite _____ grades.

2. The puppy _____(e)d from her bath much cleaner than when she entered it, but we doubted she'd stay clean for long.

3. Paul Newman is _____ not only for his acting ability, but also for his charity work.

4. My boss gave each of us such a(n) _____ bonus that I was able to buy a new sofa with the money.

5. Ella embroidered a(n) _____ design on the back of her sweatshirt. She used four colors in a complicated pattern of swirls and flowers.

6. "Gowns are so expensive," Mimi said, "that I've decided to be _____ and rent a wedding dress instead of buying one."

7. People walked past the bleeding, moaning man without even pausing; they were _____ to his need for help.

8. An Indian rain dance may seem _____ to many Americans, but it is actually more native to this country than square-dancing.

Now check your answers to these questions by turning to page 118. Going over the answers carefully will help you prepare for the next two checks, for which answers are not given.

➤ Sentence Check 2

Complete each sentence below with two words from the following list. Use each word once.

elaborate	emerge	exotic	frugal
indifferent	liberal	mediocre	notable

1-2. The actress, _____ for great acting, deserved her Academy Award. Compared to her performance, all of the others appeared _____.

3-4. Every time Sylvia shops, she manages to _____ from the store without a single foolish purchase. I wish I could be such a(n) _____ shopper.

5-6. The _____ meal, full of strange but delicious foods, involved _____ preparation that took up most of the afternoon.

7-8. Americans find it difficult to be _____ to the suffering of disaster victims, so they send _____ donations to the Red Cross when disasters strike.

➤ Final Check: A Dream About Wealth

Here is a final opportunity for you to strengthen your knowledge of the eight words. First read the following passage carefully. Then fill in each blank with a word from the box at the top of this page. (Context clues will help you figure out which word goes in which blank.) Use each word once.

When I was a very poor student, I sometimes daydreamed about being rich. I imagined being such a (1)_____ member of society that my name would turn up in the newspaper columns every time I remarried. I pictured myself traveling to (2)_____ places in faraway lands. I would forget no detail when planning (3)_____ parties for five hundred of my closest friends. There would be nothing (4)_____ in my life, not even an ordinary, average toaster. No, I would have the finest toasters, the biggest houses, the most glamorous wardrobe—the best. Of course, whenever I had the urge, I would buy diamond rings or go swimming nude in my Olympic-size pool. But I'd also be very (5)_____ in spending my money to help the poor and underprivileged. I would not be (6)_____ to their needs. After graduating, I began saving money, and I stopped daydreaming about being rich. Having some earnings to spend, I had finally (7)_____(e)d from a life of endless budgeting, a life in which I was forced to be extremely (8)_____. Of course, I am still thrifty because I don't want to waste my hard-earned money. But now that I have enough money to be comfortable, I no longer daydream about being super-rich.

> **SCORES:**   Sentence Check 2 _____ %   Final Check _____ %
> Enter your scores above and in the vocabulary performance chart on the inside back cover of the book.
>
> Number right: 8 = 100%   7 = 88%   6 = 75%   5 = 63%   4 = 50%   3 = 38%   2 = 25%   1 = 13%

Previewing the Words

Find out how many of the eight words in this chapter you already know. Try to complete each sentence with the most suitable word from the list below. Use each word once.

Leave a sentence blank rather than guessing at an answer. Your purpose here is just to get a sense of the eight words and what you may know about them.

affirm	allude	coerce	elite
essence	impair	query	sadistic

1. We are all free to the extent that no one can _____ us into holding certain beliefs.

2. Augusto will _____ the banker about the proper way to apply for a car loan.

3. Staring at the sun during an eclipse can _____ vision and even cause blindness.

4. Trust is the _____ of a good relationship; without it, the relationship won't last.

5. New U.S. Presidents _____ under oath that they will uphold the Constitution.

6. As a child, Lee was so _____ that he would smile as he pulled legs off live grasshoppers.

7. In joining the Olympic team, Kelly became a member of an _____ group of athletes.

8. Although the mayor won't name her opponent, she plans to _____ to him by mentioning the scandal in which he's involved.

Now check your answers by turning to page 118. Fix any mistakes and fill in any blank spaces by writing in the correct answers. By doing so, you will complete this introduction to the eight words.

You're now ready to strengthen your knowledge of the words you already know and to master the words you're only half sure of, or don't know at all. Turn to the next page.

Eight Words in Context

Figure out the meanings of the following eight words by looking *closely and carefully* at the context in which the words appear. Doing so will prepare you for the matching test and the practices on the two pages that follow.

1 **affirm**
(ə-fûrm')
-*verb*

   a. The witness **affirmed** in court that he had seen the defendant commit the robbery.

   b. Lana did **affirm** during the wedding ceremony that she would love and honor Joseph, but she did not state that she would obey him.

2 **allude**
(ə-lo͞od')
-*verb*

   a. In his speeches, Martin Luther King often **alluded** to the Bible's familiar stories by referring to Biblical personalities.

   b. Regina **alluded** to Sal's weight gain by calling him "Santa," instead of referring to it directly.

3 **coerce**
(kō-ûrs')
-*verb*

   a. The rebels tried to **coerce** the general into giving up by kidnapping his daughter.

   b. The Puritan colonists **coerced** Indians into slavery by capturing and selling them to buyers in the West Indies.

4 **elite**
(i-lēt')
-*adjective*

   a. The 57th was the **elite** military unit. Its members were the toughest and the smartest and had trained the longest.

   b. The **elite** neighborhood in town is surrounded by a high fence and has a guard at its gates.

5 **essence**
(es'-əns)
-*noun*

   a. New life is the **essence** of spring.

   b. The **essence** of the hour-long lecture was the idea that much important work gets done in America by volunteers.

6 **impair**
(im-pâr')
-*verb*

   a. Listening to loud music **impairs** hearing by damaging the inner ear.

   b. The rifle shot didn't kill the deer, but it **impaired** her running ability, leaving her with a limp.

7 **query**
(kwēr'-ē)
-*verb*

   a. Since no printed schedule was available, I had to **query** the man at the information booth to learn when the train would leave.

   b. Reporters repeatedly **queried** the President about taxes, but his only reply was "No comment."

8 **sadistic**
(sə-dis'-tik)
-*adjective*

   a. Instead of killing his victims quickly, the **sadistic** murderer first made them suffer.

   b. Our **sadistic** science teacher had a strange way of teaching about electrical currents: First, he had us hold hands in a circle. Then he put one student's hand on a wire with a slight electrical charge.

Matching Words and Definitions

Check your understanding of the eight words by matching each word with its definition. Look back at the sentences in "Eight Words in Context" as needed to decide on the meaning of each word.

_____ 1. **affirm**

_____ 2. **allude to**

_____ 3. **coerce**

_____ 4. **elite**

_____ 5. **essence**

_____ 6. **impair**

_____ 7. **query**

_____ 8. **sadistic**

a. to damage; weaken

b. to refer indirectly to

c. tending to take pleasure in cruelty

d. a fundamental characteristic or the most important quality of something; the heart of a matter

e. to indicate to be true

f. being or for the best, most powerful, or most privileged; superior

g. to force

h. to question; ask

CAUTION: Do not go any further until you are sure the above answers are correct. If you have studied the "Eight Words in Context," you will know how to match each word. Then you can use the matches to help you in the following practices. Your goal is to reach a point where you don't need to check definitions at all.

➤ Sentence Check 1

Complete each sentence below with the most suitable word from the box. Use each word once.

affirm	allude	coerce	elite
essence	impair	query	sadistic

1. Our gym teacher used to _____ us into doing fifty sit-ups by refusing to let anyone leave before we all had finished.

2. The _____ Nazi laughed while his victim was tortured.

3. Drugs and alcohol _____ a person's ability to drive.

4. The _____ of a paragraph is stated in its topic sentence.

5. During the spelling bee, the judge would _____ that a spelling was correct by nodding silently.

6. A(n) _____ group of doctors, including the country's top brain surgeons, met to discuss two new operations.

7. When two people are arrested for the same crime, the police _____ them separately, to see if they give the same answers.

8. My brother and I used secret names to _____ to certain relatives. For example, if we wished to speak about Aunt Dotty, we instead spoke about "an old Chevy."

Now check your answers to these questions by turning to page 118. Going over the answers carefully will help you prepare for the next two checks, for which answers are not given.

➤ Sentence Check 2

Complete each sentence below with two words from the following list. Use each word once.

affirm	allude	coerce	elite
essence	impair	query	sadistic

1-2. Our state senator would neither deny nor _____ that the _____, expensive country club he belonged to allowed no minority members.

3-4. I need to _____ my professor more closely about the chemistry theory. Although I've grasped the _____, I don't understand all the details yet.

5-6. When my roommate wants to _____ me into doing her some favor, all she has to do is _____ to certain dark secrets of mine. The hint that she might tell them is enough to make me help her out.

7-8. One terrible beating by her _____ husband was enough to _____ the woman's sight for life.

➤ Final Check: Children and Drugs

Here is a final opportunity for you to strengthen your knowledge of the eight words. First read the following passage carefully. Then fill in each blank with a word from the box at the top of this page. (Context clues will help you figure out which word goes in which blank.) Use each word once.

One of the disturbing things about drug selling is the involvement of children. Police regularly pick up pre-teens who are used as lookouts and delivery boys for drug dealers. When the police (1)_____ them, the children often say the drug dealers (2)_____ them into doing these jobs. But many poor kids are naturally attracted by the money the dealers offer. When the children speak of the dealers, they (3)_____ to them with admiration. With their fancy cars and wads of money, the dealers seem like members of a(n) (4)_____ club.

Dealers like using kids because their age protects them from serious criminal charges. The police (5)_____ that arresting the children doesn't (6)_____ the dealers' business much.

To some of the children, serving as lookouts and drug runners is almost a game. They don't realize what harm could come to them if they got involved with a really (7)_____ dealer, someone who enjoys violence. The use of these children shows that the (8)_____ of drug dealing is abuse of people.

SCORES: Sentence Check 2 _____ % Final Check _____ %
Enter your scores above and in the vocabulary performance chart on the inside back cover of the book.

Number right: 8 = 100%   7 = 88%   6 = 75%   5 = 63%   4 = 50%   3 = 38%   2 = 25%   1 = 13%

Previewing the Words

Find out how many of the eight words in this chapter you already know. Try to complete each sentence with the most suitable word from the list below. Use each word once.

Leave a sentence blank rather than guessing at an answer. Your purpose here is just to get a sense of the eight words and what you may know about them.

plausible	recur	reprimand	revoke
shrewd	skeptical	stereotype	tactic

1. The judge usually _____s a person's license for driving while drunk.

2. The county board decided that the annual fair would _____ each year during the last week in July.

3. One good _____ for getting a raise is to show your boss a list of your recent accomplishments.

4. Sandra was _____ that the fortune teller could really tell her future.

5. "When a worker breaks a rule, I give him a _____," said the strict boss. "If he breaks it again, he's fired."

6. Evan is not a _____ flea-market shopper. Instead of bargaining, he pays the full asking price, no matter how high.

7. My excuse for missing the English final did not sound _____ to my teacher. Nevertheless, my grandmother really had died, and I was attending her funeral.

8. Bev still accepts the _____ of all athletes as dumb, even though the school's star quarterback is her math tutor.

Now check your answers by turning to page 118. Fix any mistakes and fill in any blank spaces by writing in the correct answers. By doing so, you will complete this introduction to the eight words.

You're now ready to strengthen your knowledge of the words you already know and to master the words you're only half sure of, or don't know at all. Turn to the next page.

Eight Words in Context

Figure out the meanings of the following eight words by looking *closely and carefully* at the context in which the words appear. Doing so will prepare you for the matching test and the practices on the two pages that follow.

1 **plausible**
(plô'-zə-bəl)
-adjective

    a. Was Buck's excuse for being late **plausible**? Or did he tell you some unbelieveable story?

    b. "Some TV shows are just not **plausible**," said the producer. "Who ever heard of a talking horse or a flying nun?"

2 **recur**
(ri-kûr')
-verb

    a. Jordan has headaches that **recur** as often as once a day.

    b. "The labor pains are **recurring** every minute," I told the nurse. "Do you think it's about time?"

3 **reprimand**
(rep'-rə-mand')
-noun

    a. If a boss wants to blame a worker, the union requires the **reprimand** to be written.

    b. My father gave me verbal **reprimands**, but my mother would not hesitate to give me a slap on the rear end.

4 **revoke**
(ri-vōk')
-verb

    a. Mrs. Byers said she would **revoke** Ken's computer-lab privileges if he ever again squirted glue between the computer keys.

    b. To avoid having his driver's license **revoked**, Art paid the $467 for all of his speeding tickets.

5 **shrewd**
(shrōōd)
-adjective

    a. Eddie is a fine musician, but he's no good with money. So he hired a friend with a **shrewd** business sense to handle his financial affairs.

    b. Sherry is a **shrewd** flirt. She ignores men wearing a Timex watch so she'll be available for one with a Rolex.

6 **skeptical**
(skep'-ti-kəl)
-adjective

    a. Jessica's family is so rich that she is **skeptical** about any man who asks her out. She wonders if he's interested in her or in her money.

    b. I am **skeptical** about the articles on movie stars and space aliens in supermarket newspapers. My brother, however, believes every word he reads in those papers.

7 **stereotype**
(ster'-ē-ə-tīp')
-noun

    a. The used car salesman did not fit our **stereotype**. He was quiet and informative, not loud and pushy.

    b. Because all members of a group are not alike, **stereotypes** lead to inaccurate judgments of people.

8 **tactic**
(tak'-tic)
-noun

    a. The teacher finally caught on to Greg's **tactic** for getting his homework done—having his sister do it.

    b. The best **tactic** for keeping young children from fighting is to separate them.

Matching Words and Definitions

Check your understanding of the eight words by matching each word with its definition. Look back at the sentences in "Eight Words in Context" as needed to decide on the meaning of each word.

_____ 1. **plausible**   a. doubting; questioning

_____ 2. **recur**   b. clever; tricky

_____ 3. **reprimand**   c. believeable; appearing truthful or reasonable

_____ 4. **revoke**   d. to cancel or make ineffective by taking back, withdrawing, or reversing

_____ 5. **shrewd**   e. a means to reach a goal; method

_____ 6. **skeptical**   f. a harsh or formal criticism

_____ 7. **stereotype**   g. to occur again; occur over and over

_____ 8. **tactic**   h. an oversimplified image of a person or group, with no individuality taken into account

CAUTION: Do not go any further until you are sure the above answers are correct. If you have studied the "Eight Words in Context," you will know how to match each word. Then you can use the matches to help you in the following practices. Your goal is to reach a point where you don't need to check definitions at all.

➤Sentence Check 1

Complete each sentence below with the most suitable word from the box. Use each word once.

plausible	recur	reprimand	revoke
shrewd	skeptical	stereotype	tactic

1. Italian-Americans are rightly bothered by the _____ of all Italians as members of the Mafia.

2. Amber's excuse for missing the party did not seem _____. She said she was too sick, but I saw her shopping that afternoon.

3. It was _____ of Connie to move to California last year. Now she can pay in-state fees when she begins college at San Bernadino University.

4. Five-year-old Arnie's nightmare of ghosts chasing him tended to _____ at least once a week.

5. Some divorced parents who want to see more of their children use an illegal _____: kidnapping.

6. When the roofer gave us an estimate that was much lower than what others charged, we became _____ about the quality of his work.

7. The principal wrote our gym teacher a note of _____ for not having his class leave the gym right after the fire alarm rang.

8. Eleanor's parents said she could not attend the prom because of her bad grades, but later they _____(e)d the punishment and let her go anyway.

Now check your answers to these questions by turning to page 118. Going over the answers carefully will help you prepare for the next two checks, for which answers are not given.

➤Sentence Check 2

Complete each sentence below with two words from the following list. Use each word once.

plausible	recur	reprimand	revoke
shrewd	skeptical	stereotype	tactic

1-2. When it comes to preventing cheating, our science teacher is _____. His

_____s include checking our hands before a test and having us sit in alternate seats during a test.

3-4. _____s may get their start when certain behavior patterns _____ among members of a particular group.

5-6. "Of course I'm _____ of your excuse," Mel's boss said. "You have to give me a

more _____ reason for not having the sales report ready than that you couldn't find a pen or pencil."

7-8. "This time you're just getting a _____," said the judge to the owner of the hot-dog

stand. "Next time your license may be _____(e)d."

➤Final Check: Party House

Here is a final opportunity for you to strengthen your knowledge of the eight words. First read the following passage carefully. Then fill in each blank with a word from the box at the top of this page. (Context clues will help you figure out which word goes in which blank.) Use each word once.

Neighbors complained to the college about the loud parties at the Phi Gamma fraternity house, but

the Phi Gammas were (1) _____ enough to come up with a (2)_____

explanation each time. For example, they claimed that one of their members tended to have

nightmares which would (3)_____ throughout finals week, making him cry out

loudly throughout the night. This, they said, woke up all of the other members, who had gone to bed

early that evening. Again and again, the Phi Gammas were let off by the college dean with only a

(4)_____. But members of the other fraternities were (5)_____ of

Phi Gamma's excuses. They also disliked the way the group contributed to a negative

(6)_____ of fraternities. So they decided on a (7)_____ to get

back at Phi Gamma. They secretly tape-recorded one of the Phi Gamma meetings. During that

meeting, members mocked the way the dean always believed their excuses. They also made plans for

more loud parties. When the dean heard the recording, he (8)_____(e)d Phi

Gamma's campus license.

SCORES: Sentence Check 2 _____ %   **Final Check** _____ %

Enter your scores above and in the vocabulary performance chart on the inside back cover of the book.

Number right: 8 = 100%   7 = 88%   6 = 75%   5 = 63%   4 = 50%   3 = 38%   2 = 25%   1 = 13%

UNIT THREE: Test 1

PART A
Choose the word that best completes each sentence and write it in the space provided.

1. **frugal**
    liberal
    elaborate
    plausible

    It may not seem _____, but it's true—some people need only

    fifteen minutes of sleep a day.

2. **skeptical**
    passive
    indignant
    shrewd

    When the usually peppy dog became _____and wouldn't play,

    Mickey knew he must be ill.

3. **exotic**
    elite
    indifferent
    inevitable

    Hal was foolish to believe he could go steady with two women at once. It

    was _____ they would find out about each other.

4. **tactics**
    reprimands
    patrons
    rituals

    In kindergarten, an afternoon nap was required. Yet, in English class, my

    napping has earned me _____.

5. **indifferent**
    plausible
    frugal
    sadistic

    Many _____ shoppers buy soy-based foods because they are

    inexpensive sources of protein.

6. **notable**
    mediocre
    exotic
    elite

    The singer's voice is only _____, but he's very popular

    because his personality is so appealing.

7. **ritual**
    stereotype
    query
    patron

    For an Arab Moslem man, the entire divorce _____ consists

    of announcing to his wife before two witnesses, "I divorce you."

8. **refuted**
    coerced
    emerged
    affirmed

    Experts have _____ the idea that giant redwood trees are the

    oldest living things on Earth. Some pine trees, aged about 4,600 years, are now
    known to be older.

9. **exiles**
    stereotypes
    essences
    options

    We considered several _____ for dinner: cooking, going out,

    or having a pizza delivered.

10. **adapt**
    dismay
    query
    allude

    My teacher meant to _____, "Why did you miss the history

    lecture?" Instead he asked, "Why did you hiss the mystery lecture?"

(Continues on next page)

PART B
Circle C if the italicized word is used **correctly**. Circle I if the word is used **incorrectly**.

C I 11. Gina and Steve are *patrons* of the local Japanese restaurant. They eat there every Friday night.

C I 12. *Elite* members of our society include homeless people and AIDS victims.

C I 13. The *sadistic* herring gull gives a special call that invites other gulls to share its food.

C I 14. As a *gesture* of respect, my boyfriend makes a point of greeting my parents and grandmother whenever he comes to call for me.

C I 15. Although most *notable* as a scientist, Albert Einstein was also well known as a spokesman for world peace.

C I 16. Before eyeglasses were invented, some people whose vision was *impaired* looked through clear gemstones shaped like lenses.

C I 17. The Liberty Bell, so *exotic* to all Americans, was once offered for sale as scrap metal.

C I 18. If you're entering a movie theater with a crowd, it's *shrewd* to bear left. Since most people head right, you'll get a better choice of seats that way.

C I 19. The old belief that men prefer blonde women to brunettes was *affirmed* by a poll of college students: Most males liked brunettes better than blondes.

C I 20. Marie always thinks handsome men are nice. She seems to *equate* good looks with good character.

SCORE: (Number correct) _____ x 5 = _____ %

Enter your scores above and in the vocabulary performance chart on the inside back cover of the book.

UNIT THREE: Test 2

PART A
Complete each sentence with a word from the box. Use each word once.

adapt	coerce	elaborate	essence	exile
reciprocated	recur	retained	stereotype	tactic

1. After my brother gave me the measles, I _____ by giving him the mumps.

2. The _____ dollhouse included many realistic details, such as tiny lamps, clocks, and flowers in vases.

3. The _____ of a thunderstorm is energy—energy sometimes equal to that of a dozen atomic bombs.

4. Although mono doesn't generally _____ in the same individual, some people do get the disease more than once.

5. The _____ of the cowboy is of a rough and romantic fighter, but most cowboys spent their days working steadily at a series of routine chores.

6. A native author had to leave China to avoid being imprisoned. He was forced into

    _____ for attacking the Chinese government in his writings.

7. Trained dogs help deaf people _____ to a silent world by alerting them to the sounds of such things as doorbells and smoke alarms.

8. Many students have used the _____ of blaming the computer for their missed deadlines. They say, for example, "It erased my whole paper."

9. Built of white marble and decorated with gems, the famous Taj Mahal of India has

    _____ its beauty for more than three hundred years.

10. Because a thief might _____ you into handing over a wallet, carry an extra one with little money, an old ID card, and out-of-date credit cards.

(Continues on next page)

PART B
Circle C if the italicized word is used **correctly.** Circle I if the word is used **incorrectly.**

C   I   11.   Judging by the smile of relief on his face, the X-ray *dismayed* Dr. Fry.

C   I   12.   I was *skeptical* when the salesman said I could get a month's worth of frozen food for under fifty dollars a person.

C   I   13.   People who get around in wheelchairs are bound to be *indifferent* to a new wheelchair that follows spoken instructions.

C   I   14.   According to a study, most working couples spend a *liberal* amount of time talking with their children—on average, less than a minute a day.

C   I   15.   The poem *alludes* to so many 18th-century events that it is difficult for today's readers to get its full meaning.

C   I   16.   The construction company had its building license *revoked* when its materials were found to be dangerously weak.

C   I   17.   Bob *endeavored* to save the diseased tree, saying, "Let's just chop it down for firewood."

C   I   18.   My sister *imposes* on her husband's good nature by having him run errands for her all the time.

C   I   19.   Having recently lent Trisha money, I was *indignant* when I learned she had spent it on an expensive vacation instead of clothes for her children.

C   I   20.   Every day, the original Declaration of Independence is on display in a glass case. Every evening, however, it *emerges* into an underground container that resists extreme heat or cold, water, fire, and explosions.

> *SCORE:* (Number correct) _____ x 5 = _____ %

Enter your scores above and in the vocabulary performance chart on the inside back cover of the book.

UNIT THREE: Test 3

In the space provided, write the letter of the choice that is most nearly the **same** in meaning as the boldfaced word.

_____ 1. **ritual**   a) sign   b) adjustment   c) ceremony   d) wealth

_____ 2. **patron**   a) customer   b) employer   c) voter   d) owner

_____ 3. **coerce**   a) force   b) join   c) deny   d) support

_____ 4. **impose on**   a) uninterested in   b) keep   c) take advantage of   d) take away from

_____ 5. **endeavor**   a) repay   b) try   c) leave   d) repeat

_____ 6. **option**   a) main quality   b) question   c) method   d) choice

_____ 7. **adapt**   a) disprove   b) consider equal   c) adjust   d) inform

_____ 8. **reprimand**   a) criticism   b) repetition   c) separation   d) reminder

_____ 9. **reciprocate**   a) repeat   b) approve   c) repay   d) keep

_____ 10. **equate**   a) multiply   b) consider equal   c) appear   d) force

_____ 11. **gesture**   a) question   b) method   c) doubt   d) action showing one's attitude

_____ 12. **recur**   a) happen again   b) pay back   c) discourage   d) respect

_____ 13. **allude**   a) mislead   b) refer indirectly   c) make ineffective   d) attract

_____ 14. **exile**   a) equality   b) harm   c) separation from home   d) travel

_____ 15. **refute**   a) support   b) disprove   c) admit   d) refuse

_____ 16. **tactic**   a) effort   b) criticism   c) central quality   d) method

_____ 17. **indignant**   a) angry   b) cruel   c) doubtful   d) generous

_____ 18. **essence**   a) protection   b) question   c) search   d) heart of a matter

_____ 19. **shrewd**   a) clear   b) simple   c) clever   d) stupid

_____ 20. **stereotype**   a) alternative   b) oversimplified image   c) ceremony   d) effort

(Continues on next page)

PART B: Antonyms
In the space provided, write the letter of the choice that is most nearly the **opposite** in meaning to the boldfaced word.

_____ 21. **skeptical**   a) respectful   b) equal   c) dull   d) convinced

_____ 22. **emerge**   a) disappear   b) improve   c) appear   d) harm

_____ 23. **liberal**   a) simple   b) clever   c) cheap   d) pleased

_____ 24. **elaborate**   a) foreign   b) uninterested   c) kind   d) simple

_____ 25. **frugal**   a) wasteful   b) special   c) ordinary   d) angry

_____ 26. **notable**   a) complicated   b) unknown   c) excellent   d) active

_____ 27. **retain**   a) admit   b) give away   c) contain   d) take advantage of

_____ 28. **query**   a) appear   b) admire   c) refer   d) answer

_____ 29. **affirm**   a) happen once   b) deny   c) separate   d) support

_____ 30. **passive**   a) known   b) generous   c) ordinary   d) active

_____ 31. **impair**   a) double   b) reverse   c) improve   d) answer

_____ 32. **elite**   a) worst   b) foreign   c) natural   d) playful

_____ 33. **inevitable**   a) unknown   b) believable   c) avoidable   d) simple

_____ 34. **dismay**   a) encourage   b) disprove   c) disappoint   d) find

_____ 35. **mediocre**   a) active   b) pleased   c) excellent   d) unbelievable

_____ 36. **indifferent**   a) odd   b) interested   c) ordinary   d) disappointed

_____ 37. **sadistic**   a) happy   b) angry   c) wealthy   d) kind

_____ 38. **plausible**   a) unbelievable   b) avoidable   c) unknown   d) thrifty

_____ 39. **exotic**   a) best   b) worst   c) commonplace   d) unusual

_____ 40. **revoke**   a) state clearly   b) remind   c) make effective   d) prove

SCORE: (Number correct) _____ x 2.5 = _____ %

Enter your scores above and in the vocabulary performance chart on the inside back cover of the book.

UNIT THREE: *Test 4*

PART A
Complete each sentence in a way that clearly shows you understand the meaning of the boldfaced word. Take a minute to plan your answer before you write.

Example: A **mediocre** essay is likely to _____ *receive a grade of C.* _____

1. Lonnie needs to get from New York to Florida. One of his **options** is to _____

_____

2. A cab driver might respond to a **liberal** tip by _____

_____

3. When the heater broke, I **adapted** to the sudden drop in temperature by _____

_____

4. One good **tactic** for dieting is _____

_____

5. When Gina invited Daniel out for coffee, he **reciprocated** by_____

_____

6. An animal-lover would become **indignant** if_____

_____

7. A **shrewd** shopper will probably spend a lot of time _____

_____

8. My mother always used to give me this **reprimand**: " _____

_____

9. One **exotic** place I'd like to visit some day is _____

_____

10. A **skeptical** response to "I love you" is " _____

_____

(Continues on next page)

PART B

After each boldfaced word are a *synonym* (a word that means the same as the boldfaced word), an *antonym* (a word that means the opposite of the boldfaced word), and a word that is neither. Mark the synonym with an *S* and the antonym with an *A*.

Example: **plausible**   _S_ believable   _A_ doubtful   _____ soft

11-12. **retain**   _____ lose   _____ keep   _____ limit

13-14. **frugal**   _____ hasty   _____ wasteful   _____ thrifty

15-16. **elaborate** _____ orderly   _____ complicated _____ simple

17-18. **impair**   _____ weaken   _____ call   _____ strengthen

19-20. **elite**   _____ lowest   _____ best   _____ heavy

PART C

Use five of the following ten words in sentences. Make it clear that you know the meaning of the word you use. Feel free to use the past tense or plural form of a word.

coerce	emerge	equate	gesture	indifferent
passive	recur	ritual	sadistic	stereotype

21. _____

_____

22. _____

_____

23. _____

_____

24. _____

_____

25. _____

SCORE: (Number correct) _____ x 4 = _____ %

Enter your scores above and in the vocabulary performance chart on the inside back cover of the book.

Unit Four

Previewing the Words

Find out how many of the eight words in this chapter you already know. Try to complete each sentence with the most suitable word from the list below. Use each word once.

Leave a sentence blank rather than guessing at an answer. Your purpose here is just to get a sense of the eight words and what you may know about them.

consequence	destiny	detain	diminish
procrastinate	tedious	transaction	vital

1. Because Carrie left out a _____ ingredient, the apple cake came out looking like a pancake.

2. Susanna forgot to buy milk. As a _____, she had to wash down dry cereal with her coffee the next morning.

3. When it comes to housework, it pays to _____ for a week. Then the next week, you can do two weeks' worth of cleaning at once.

4. "May I _____ you one minute, for some directions?" asked a stranger as I hurried to work.

5. Using an automatic bank machine takes less time than a _____ with a human bank teller.

6. Shakespeare wrote that Romeo and Juliet's _____ is written in the stars, but I don't believe in fate.

7. Beth hoped her headache would _____ after she took two aspirins, but it didn't lessen at all.

8. _____ chores, like washing dishes, are less boring if you do them while you listen to the radio or talk with a friend.

Now check your answers by turning to page 119. Fix any mistakes and fill in any blank spaces by writing in the correct answers. By doing so, you will complete this introduction to the eight words.

You're now ready to strengthen your knowledge of the words you already know and to master the words you're only half sure of, or don't know at all. Turn to the next page.

Eight Words in Context

Figure out the meanings of the following eight words by looking *closely and carefully* at the context in which the words appear. Doing so will prepare you for the matching test and the practices on the two pages that follow.

1 **consequence**
(kon'-si-kwens)
-noun

   a. As a **consequence** of her heavy spending at the mall, Lily was short of cash until her next paycheck.

   b. When children reach for something hot or sharp, it's because they don't know the **consequences** of such actions.

2 **destiny**
(des'-tə-nē)
-noun

   a. Believing in fate, the soldier wondered if his **destiny** was to die in the coming battle.

   b. Marc believes much of his life is set by **destiny**. For example, he feels that he and Debbie were born for each other.

3 **detain**
(di-tān')
-verb

   a. Paul's history teacher **detained** him after class to speak privately about his surprisingly low test results.

   b. **Detained** at home by a friend in urgent need of advice, Gloria was late for work.

4 **diminish**
(di-min'-ish)
-verb

   a. After Mother yelled, "Turn that thing down!" the sound from the stereo **diminished** from a roar to a soft hum.

   b. As the cost of living rises, the value of a person's life savings **diminishes**.

5 **procrastinate**
(prə-kras'-tə-nāt')
-verb

   a. Morgan **procrastinated** so long that when she finally returned the dress to the store, it was too late for a refund.

   b. I can't **procrastinate** any longer. I must study tonight because the final exam is tomorrow morning.

6 **tedious**
(tē'-dē-əs)
-adjective

   a. Is anything more **tedious** than lugging a heavy sack of clothes to a laundromat and then waiting forever for the laundry to be done?

   b. John found the homework assignment very **tedious**; the questions were dull and repetitious.

7 **transaction**
(tran-sak'-shən)
-noun

   a. A police officer spotted the **transaction** between the drug dealer and an addict.

   b. Among some business people, a **transaction** is finalized with a handshake. These business deals are never put in writing.

8 **vital**
(vīt'-l)
-adjective

   a. Water is **vital** to the survival of all living things.

   b. For Teresa to pass her math course, it is **vital** that she pass the final exam.

Matching Words and Definitions

Check your understanding of the eight words by matching each word with its definition. Look back at the sentences in "Eight Words in Context" as needed to decide on the meaning of each word.

_____ 1. **consequence**

_____ 2. **destiny**

_____ 3. **detain**

_____ 4. **diminish**

_____ 5. **procrastinate**

_____ 6. **tedious**

_____ 7. **transaction**

_____ 8. **vital**

a. to lessen or become smaller

b. a result

c. a business deal or action; exchange of money, goods, or services

d. necessary; important

e. boring; uninteresting because of great length, slowness, or repetition

f. delay; to keep from continuing

g. to put off doing something until later

h. fate; an unavoidable occurrence

CAUTION: Do not go any further until you are sure the above answers are correct. If you have studied the "Eight Words in Context," you will know how to match each word. Then you can use the matches to help you in the following practices. Your goal is to reach a point where you don't need to check definitions at all.

➣ *Sentence Check 1*

Complete each sentence below with the most suitable word from the box. Use each word once.

consequence	destiny	detain	diminish
procrastinate	tedious	transaction	vital

1. The _____ at the checkout counter was delayed by an incorrect price label.

2. The afternoon sunshine caused the snowman's height to _____ from six feet to three.

3. To _____ is to follow the old saying, "Never do today what you can put off until tomorrow."

4. As a _____ of his staying out too late, Wilson wasn't allowed out for a week.

5. After his wife died in a fire, Ryan felt such tragedies are decided by _____. He refused to believe her death was meaningless.

6. The secret agent paid for information he thought was _____ to our national safety, but he had been tricked into buying useless knowledge.

7. "If my science teacher didn't _____ us past the bell every day, I wouldn't be late for my next class," explained George.

8. To make raking autumn leaves less _____, my sister and I took turns jumping into the newly created piles.

Now check your answers to these questions by turning to page 119. Going over the answers carefully will help you prepare for the next two checks, for which answers are not given.

➤ Sentence Check 2

Complete each sentence below with two words from the following list. Use each word once.

consequence	destiny	detain	diminish
procrastinate	tedious	transaction	vital

1-2. "I'm sorry to _____ you," the salesman said, "but any _____ involving payment with a personal check takes longer than a cash purchase."

3-4. The _____ of poor nutrition is illness. A balanced diet is _____ for health.

5-6. Unfortunately, it doesn't help to _____ in paying your bills—putting them off doesn't make them _____ or disappear.

7-8. "This job is so _____ I'm afraid I'll die of boredom," said the file clerk. "Is it my _____ to put things in alphabetical order for the rest of my life?"

➤ Final Check: Procrastinator

Here is a final opportunity for you to strengthen your knowledge of the eight words. First read the following passage carefully. Then fill in each blank with a word from the box at the top of this page. (Context clues will help you figure out which word goes in which blank.) Use each word once.

One of these days there is going to be a "new me": I will no longer (1)_____. I'm making this my New Year's resolution. Well, yes, I know it's March. I was going to make this resolution in January, but all that Christmas shopping and cookie-baking (2)_____(e)d me. In February I figured out a way to help me stop putting things off, and I'll get around to it soon because I know that it's (3)_____ for me to change my ways. My problem is that some jobs are so (4)_____ that just thinking of them makes me want to yawn. But I know that the (5)_____ of putting things off is that nothing actually gets done. And once I get started on my New Year's resolution, my tendency to delay things will surely gradually (6)_____. I'll finish every household project and financial (7)_____ that I start. Maybe I'll even make a list of activities I can do at the same time, such as sewing while watching TV, or cleaning my junk drawer while I talk to my mother on the phone. I'd make a list now if I could just find a pen. I was going to buy pens yesterday, but I figured I'd be at the mall on Friday, so why make a special trip? I'll make the list later. Oh well, maybe it's just my (8)_____ to put things off.

SCORES: Sentence Check 2 _____ %   Final Check _____ %
Enter your scores above and in the vocabulary performance chart on the inside back cover of the book.

Number right: 8 = 100%   7 = 88%   6 = 75%   5 = 63%   4 = 50%   3 = 38%   2 = 25%   1 = 13%

17

Previewing the Words

Find out how many of the eight words in this chapter you already know. Try to complete each sentence with the most suitable word from the list below. Use each word once.

Leave a sentence blank rather than guessing at an answer. Your purpose here is just to get a sense of the eight words and what you may know about them.

discriminate	dismal	dispense	profound
severity	site	subside	vocation

1. Women now take on many _____s once thought to be mainly for men, including carpentry and firefighting.

2. The _____ of the judge's sentence—death by hanging—shocked the family of the defendant.

3. Billy Joel stepped onto the stage, and the audience's cheering didn't _____ for ten minutes.

4. The _____ of the future library was only a block from the present library.

5. Martin Luther King's "I Have a Dream" speech had a _____ effect on me. I still cry whenever I hear it.

6. Andy's favorite gift on his fifth birthday was a machine that would _____ a gumball when a penny was put in.

7. Jessica, tone deaf, can't _____ between good music and bad. To her, a song by Stevie Wonder is barely more satisfying than one by a local band.

8. This room is too _____. It needs a party to brighten it up.

Now check your answers by turning to page 119. Fix any mistakes and fill in any blank spaces by writing in the correct answers. By doing so, you will complete this introduction to the eight words.

You're now ready to strengthen your knowledge of the words you already know and to master the words you're only half sure of, or don't know at all. Turn to the next page.

Eight Words in Context

Figure out the meanings of the following eight words by looking *closely and carefully* at the context in which the words appear. Doing so will prepare you for the matching test and the practices on the two pages that follow.

1 **discriminate**
(di-skrim'-ə-nāt')
-verb

    a. It's easy to **discriminate** between frozen and fresh vegetables—fresh taste much better.

    b. Tests show that women tend to **discriminate** better among colors than men. Cherry red, cranberry red, and purplish red are all simply dark red to many men.

2 **dismal**
(diz'-məl)
-adjective

    a. Most New York subway stations are **dismal** compared to the cheerful stations in Washington, D.C.

    b. "It is a **dismal**, rainy day," Mona told her disappointed children. "But we don't have to cancel the picnic—we can have it on the kitchen floor."

3 **dispense**
(di-spens')
-verb

    a. The broken soda machine **dispensed** either a cup or soda, but not both together.

    b. Restroom soap holders that are supposed to **dispense** liquid soap at each pull seem to be empty most of the time.

4 **profound**
(prə-found')
-adjective

    a. The death of a spouse can cause **profound** depression that, in some cases, can even lead to the death of the partner.

    b. Ever since her stepfather slapped her mother, Stacy has had a **profound** hatred of him.

5 **severity**
(sə-ver'-ə-tē)
-noun

    a. The **severity** of the fire could be seen in the burnt, smoking ruins of the once beautiful building.

    b. Mark believes the **severity** of his punishment was too great. A hundred hours of weekend trash cleanup seemed too harsh a penalty for throwing two Coke cans onto the highway.

6 **site**
(sīt)
-noun

    a. The oldest private home in the New England town was named an historical **site**.

    b. Wounded Knee, S.D., is the **site** of a 1971 conflict between the federal government and the Sioux Indians.

7 **subside**
(səb-sīd')
-verb

    a. When I'm really furious, a walk around the block helps the anger **subside**.

    b. Consuela sat in the car until the storm **subsided**. Then she dashed up the sidewalk and into school.

8 **vocation**
(vō-kā'-shən)
-noun

    a. Raising German shepherds was just a hobby for Louise. Her **vocation** was library science.

    b. If you can't decide on a career, you might wish to take a test that reveals which **vocations** you're suited for.

Matching Words and Definitions

Check your understanding of the eight words by matching each word with its definition. Look back at the sentences in "Eight Words in Context" as needed to decide on the meaning of each word.

_____ 1. **discriminate**   a. deeply felt or realized

_____ 2. **dismal**   b. to see the difference(s); distinguish

_____ 3. **dispense**   c. the spot where a place or event was, is, or will be located

_____ 4. **profound**   d. a profession or occupation

_____ 5. **severity**   e. gloomy; cheerless; depressing

_____ 6. **site**   f. to give out in portions or amounts

_____ 7. **subside**   g. a harshness; intensity; seriousness; harmful extent

_____ 8. **vocation**   h. to become less active; calm down; become less in amount or degree

CAUTION: Do not go any further until you are sure the above answers are correct. If you have studied the "Eight Words in Context," you will know how to match each word. Then you can use the matches to help you in the following practices. Your goal is to reach a point where you don't need to check definitions at all.

➤ *Sentence Check 1*

Complete each sentence below with the most suitable word from the box. Use each word once.

discriminate	dismal	dispense	profound
severity	site	subside	vocation

1. Most people cannot _____ between an alligator and a crocodile.

2. Today there is a _____ interest in the rights of animals.

3. The waves were enormous in the bay, but they began to _____ as the boat moved out into open water.

4. Among the most dangerous _____s are deep-sea diving, mining, and construction.

5. Kyle was annoyed by the _____ news that mono would keep him out of college for a whole semester.

6. Do you think food machines at public schools should _____ only nutritious foods, such as fruit and juices?

7. Medication should match the _____ of an illness. For example, a powerful medicine isn't needed for a cold.

8. Although the _____ where the hiker claimed a spaceship had landed was burned, no one believed him.

Now check your answers to these questions by turning to page 119. Going over the answers carefully will help you prepare for the next two checks, for which answers are not given.

➤ *Sentence Check 2*

Complete each sentence below with two words from the following list. Use each word once.

discriminate	dismal	dispense	profound
severity	site	subside	vocation

1-2. My visit to the school for retarded children had a _____ effect on me. I knew that day

that my _____ would be in special education.

3-4. It was not until I was ten miles away from the _____ of the accident that my shaking

began to _____ .

5-6. The movie was meant to be a dark comedy, but I found it to be _____. I often

couldn't _____ between lines that were meant to be funny and lines that were just
depressing.

7-8. Some hospitals now allow patients to judge the _____ of their own pain and to

_____ small amounts of medication to themselves as necessary.

➤ *Final Check:* Changes in View

Here is a final opportunity for you to strengthen your knowledge of the eight words. First read the following
passage carefully. Then fill in each blank with a word from the box at the top of this page. (Context clues will
help you figure out which word goes in which blank.) Use each word once.

What an education I got yesterday! I am studying to be a nurse. Part of my preparation for this
(1)_____ involves training in a mental hospital. When I went there yesterday, I was
scared. I imagined (2)_____, dark rooms where people sat staring and drooling. I
pictured screaming patients who might even try to hurt me. But yesterday my views of mental
hospitals went through a (3)_____ change. First of all, the (4)_____
of the hospital is at the edge of a lovely small town, and its grounds are green and neat. When I arrived
there, I was brought to a big, cheerful room where patients were talking, playing ping-pong or cards,
or doing craft projects.

I spoke to one patient. She seemed like a nice, normal person who happened to have problems.
She told me her illness had been of much greater (5)_____ when she first came to
this hospital. At that time, she could not always (6)_____ between what was real
and what she imagined. Like many patients, she was often upset and confused. But the doctors put her
on medicine, which the nurses still (7)_____ three times a day. The medicine, as
well as talks with the doctors, nurses and other patients, have helped her illness
(8)_____. Perhaps our conversation was helpful to her; I know it helped me. Now
I'm thinking about working in the mental health field after I get my nursing degree.

SCORES: Sentence Check 2 _____ %	Final Check _____ %

Enter your scores above and in the vocabulary performance chart on the inside back cover of the book.

Number right: 8 = 100%   7 = 88%   6 = 75%   5 = 63%   4 = 50%   3 = 38%   2 = 25%   1 = 13%

Previewing the Words

Find out how many of the eight words in this chapter you already know. Try to complete each sentence with the most suitable word from the list below. Use each word once.

Leave a sentence blank rather than guessing at an answer. Your purpose here is just to get a sense of the eight words and what you may know about them.

data	innate	intervene	morbid
obstinate	parallel	perceptive	sedate

1. My two-year-old son is so _____ that he refuses to eat his dinner without his Mickey Mouse spoon.

2. _____ people can often know what we are thinking just by looking at us.

3. Before Phyllis can finish her research paper on acid rain, she needs to collect more

   _____ on its effects.

4. "All of this talk of sickness and death is too _____ for me," Blake said. "Let's talk about something more cheerful."

5. When two children get into a fight, it is sometimes best not to _____ but to let them work it out themselves.

6. At four, Sandra could already multiply. Since her talent for math showed up at such an early age, it

   must be _____.

7. The railroad workers laid the track carefully, making sure the rails were _____, exactly the same distance apart at every point.

8. On the roller coaster, most of us screamed with excitement and fear. In contrast, Michael somehow

   was able to look _____.

Now check your answers by turning to page 119. Fix any mistakes and fill in any blank spaces by writing in the correct answers. By doing so, you will complete this introduction to the eight words.

You're now ready to strengthen your knowledge of the words you already know and to master the words you're only half sure of, or don't know at all. Turn to the next page.

Eight Words in Context

Figure out the meanings of the following eight words by looking *closely and carefully* at the context in which the words appear. Doing so will prepare you for the matching test and the practices on the two pages that follow.

1 **data**
(dā'-tə)
-*noun*

   a. Jodi considers the available **data** on a car—including its fuel economy, safety, and repair record—before deciding whether to buy it.

   b. Jane Goodall collected important **data** on chimpanzees by observing their behavior in the wild.

2 **innate**
(i-nāt')
-*adjective*

   a. Rick's musical ability must be **innate** because even as an infant he could play the piano by ear and make up his own tunes.

   b. Psychologists try to learn how many of our abilities and interests are **innate** and how many of them we gain through experience.

3 **intervene**
(in'-tər-vēn')
-*verb*

   a. The two boxers would have killed each other if the referee hadn't finally decided to **intervene**.

   b. When my parents argue, I get out of the way rather than trying to **intervene**.

4 **morbid**
(môr'-bid)
-*adjective*

   a. Great comedians can make even as **morbid** a topic as murder or terrorism a source of laughter.

   b. The movie, about people dying of cancer, was so **morbid** I felt gloomy for hours after seeing it.

5 **obstinate**
(ob'-stə-nit)
-*adjective*

   a. No matter how I prodded, Andrew remained **obstinate**; he refused to move out of the city.

   b. My father has a reputation for being **obstinate**. But he never insists on having his own way with his sister, who is even more stubborn.

6 **parallel**
(par'-ə-lel')
-*adjective*

   a. On Jeff's first bookcase, the shelves weren't **parallel**—they were two inches closer on the left than on the right.

   b. **Parallel** lines run alongside each other but never meet.

7 **perceptive**
(pər-sep'-tiv)
-*adjective*

   a. Children are more **perceptive** than many people think. They can usually sense their parents' moods and know whether or not it is a good time to ask for something.

   b. Professor Banks is especially **perceptive** when it comes to her students. She always seems to know which ones are under special stress.

8 **sedate**
(si-dāt')
-*adjective*

   a. While the officer wrote out the ticket, Beverly remained **sedate** and even wished the officer a pleasant day. But after he left, she pounded the steering wheel and loudly cursed the police force.

   b. As an experienced surgeon, Dr. Greenbaum remains **sedate** even in an emergency, performing the most complicated operations with complete calm.

Matching Words and Definitions

Check your understanding of the eight words by matching each word with its definition. Look back at the sentences in "Eight Words in Context" as needed to decide on the meaning of each word.

_____ 1. **data**   a. to come in or between for some purpose

_____ 2. **innate**   b. calm; serious and unemotional

_____ 3. **intervene**   c. the same distance apart at every point along a length

_____ 4. **morbid**   d. understanding and insightful; observant; aware

_____ 5. **obstinate**   e. information gathered for a study or a decision

_____ 6. **parallel**   f. possessed at birth; inborn

_____ 7. **perceptive**   g. causing horror or disgust

_____ 8. **sedate**   h. stubborn

CAUTION: Do not go any further until you are sure the above answers are correct. If you have studied the "Eight Words in Context," you will know how to match each word. Then you can use the matches to help you in the following practices. Your goal is to reach a point where you don't need to check definitions at all.

➤ *Sentence Check 1*

Complete each sentence below with the most suitable word from the box. Use each word once.

data	innate	intervene	morbid
obstinate	parallel	perceptive	sedate

1. For his psychology experiment, Rudy is gathering _____ to show which memory aids work best for students.

2. Since his father died, Fred's conversation is often _____, overly concerned with such gloomy topics as funerals and death.

3. While my dog gets excited easily, my cat remains _____ even when everyone around her is in a whirl of activity.

4. Kwan is so _____ that she often correctly judges a person's character after a brief conversation.

5. When you frame a picture, the picture's edges should be _____ to those of the frame, not dipping down or slanting up.

6. The referee had to _____ and separate the two hockey players, who had started hitting each other.

7. I tried to convince my son to join the family for dinner, but he was _____, refusing to leave his room no matter what I said.

8. Richard's gift for fixing machines seems _____. Even as a child, he could take one look at a broken machine and know what was wrong with it.

Now check your answers to these questions by turning to page 119. Going over the answers carefully will help you prepare for the next two checks, for which answers are not given.

➤Sentence Check 2

Complete each sentence below with two words from the following list. Use each word once.

data	innate	intervene	morbid
obstinate	parallel	perceptive	sedate

1-2. As a child, Calvin was _____, rarely excited or upset. As a teenager, however, he is

   often angry and _____—so stubborn that he hates to change his mind.

3-4. Angie's work is quite _____. She collects _____ on all the serious
   diseases and the top ten causes of death.

5-6. Jason's math ability must be _____—by age two he could add and subtract, and by

   age seven he could tell whether two lines were _____ without even using a ruler.

7-8. A good marriage counselor, _____ enough to understand both the husband's and the

   wife's points of view, doesn't _____ in the couple's arguments, but helps them decide
   how to solve their problems themselves.

➤Final Check: Family Differences

Here is a final opportunity for you to strengthen your knowledge of the eight words. First read the following passage carefully. Then fill in each blank with a word from the box at the top of this page. (Context clues will help you figure out which word goes in which blank.) Use each word once.

   I am always amazed at how different all of my brothers and sisters are. Sheila, who succeeds at everything she tries, has no patience with the rest of us. She thinks that it's up to her to (1)_____ in what we do so that things will be done the right way—her way. Jack, on the other hand, is very (2)_____. He doesn't let anything bother him, and so he rarely loses his temper. Chris is the one who never gives in. As a baby, he was already so (3)_____ that he would spit food he didn't like right at my mother. Stacey, the most social, likes people and seems to have an (4)_____ ability to make them feel good. She has always been very (5)_____, knowing just what mood others were in and what they might need. Frank has always seemed a little sad. While the rest of us kids would be riding bikes or jumping ropes, he would be doing something (6)_____, like holding a funeral for a dead frog or bird. Betty has the quickest mind of us all. When she was just four, she told my dad, "Those two shelves aren't (7)_____—the books are farther apart on the left than on the right." By age six, she was collecting (8)_____ for a book she was writing on insects. Yes, my brothers and sisters are all different. They may be strange at times, but they're never boring.

SCORES: Sentence Check 2 _____ %   **Final Check** _____ %
Enter your scores above and in the vocabulary performance chart on the inside back cover of the book.

Number right: 8 = 100%   7 = 88%   6 = 75%   5 = 63%   4 = 50%   3 = 38%   2 = 25%   1 = 13%

Previewing the Words

Find out how many of the eight words in this chapter you already know. Try to complete each sentence with the most suitable word from the list below. Use each word once.

Leave a sentence blank rather than guessing at an answer. Your purpose here is just to get a sense of the eight words and what you may know about them.

confirm	deceptive	defy	restrain
submit	susceptible	valid	vigorous

1. In a courtroom, gossip isn't considered _____ testimony—it's too unreliable.

2. Maya called the airline to _____ her flight reservation before she drove to the airport.

3. Any prisoner who dared to _____ the guards was badly beaten.

4. Because Lenny refused to _____ to his grandfather's wishes, he was removed from the will.

5. Fran is so _____ to blushing that she turns away whenever she is embarrassed, so no one will see her turn red.

6. The little boy tried to _____ his big dog from chasing a car, but he could not hold the dog back.

7. The seeming ease with which Nadia plays the piano is _____; she practices hours each day.

8. My 80-year-old grandmother is still _____ enough to walk four miles every day.

Now check your answers by turning to page 119. Fix any mistakes and fill in any blank spaces by writing in the correct answers. By doing so, you will complete this introduction to the eight words.

You're now ready to strengthen your knowledge of the words you already know and to master the words you're only half sure of, or don't know at all. Turn to the next page.

Eight Words in Context

Figure out the meanings of the following eight words by looking *closely and carefully* at the context in which the words appear. Doing so will prepare you for the matching test and the practices on the two pages that follow.

1 **confirm**
(kən-fûrm')
-*verb*

   a. Because his doctor's appointment had been made weeks before, Daniel phoned to **confirm** the date and time.

   b. "Yes, it's true," the union leader said, **confirming** the report that the teachers would refuse to do lunch duty from now on.

2 **deceptive**
(di-sep'-tiv)
-*adjective*

   a. Certain car mirrors are **deceptive**. They make other cars seem farther away than they really are.

   b. After stealing the radio, Meg remained silent while another student was wrongly accused. Her silence was as **deceptive** as an outright lie.

3 **defy**
(di-fī')
-*verb*

   a. The automotive plant workers voted to **defy** the company and go on strike.

   b. After being forbidden to go out three evenings in a row, Ted **defied** his parents by walking right out the front door.

4 **restrain**
(ri-strān')
-*verb*

   a. I **restrained** myself from laughing when my brother made a funny face while Uncle William told us—yet again—the story of his operation.

   b. Larry was so angry that we had to **restrain** him by force from punching Neal.

5 **submit**
(səb-mit')
-*verb*

   a. After bucking wildly for several minutes, the horse calmed down and **submitted** to the rider.

   b. For safety reasons, travelers must **submit** to being inspected at airports.

6 **susceptible**
(sə-sep'-tə-bəl)
-*adjective*

   a. Some people view falling in love as an illness to which romantic people are especially **susceptible**.

   b. People who smoke are more **susceptible** to colds than others.

7 **valid**
(val'-id)
-*adjective*

   a. The research study was not **valid** because the researcher had lied about the facts, which really did not support his conclusion.

   b. "Your accusation that I'm not responsible isn't **valid**," Mona told her father. "I've done all my homework already and even cleaned the living room."

8 **vigorous**
(vig'-ər-əs)
-*adjective*

   a. Joanie is so **vigorous** that she constantly needs to release energy. She often roller-skates for hours at a time.

   b. The best teachers have **vigorous** personalities. They are lively enough to make any lesson interesting.

Matching Words and Definitions

Check your understanding of the eight words by matching each word with its definition. Look back at the sentences in "Eight Words in Context" as needed to decide on the meaning of each word.

_____ 1. **confirm**	a. likely to be affected by; likely to be stricken with
_____ 2. **deceptive**	b. misleading; intended or intending to deceive
_____ 3. **defy**	c. to boldly oppose; openly resist; stand up to
_____ 4. **restrain**	d. to check or establish that something is true or correct; support the truth of something
_____ 5. **submit**	e. firmly based on facts or logic; logical; well grounded
_____ 6. **susceptible to**	f. lively; energetic
_____ 7. **valid**	g. to give in to another's power or authority
_____ 8. **vigorous**	h. to hold back from action

CAUTION: Do not go any further until you are sure the above answers are correct. If you have studied the "Eight Words in Context," you will know how to match each word. Then you can use the matches to help you in the following practices. Your goal is to reach a point where you don't need to check definitions at all.

➤*Sentence Check 1*

Complete each sentence below with the most suitable word from the box. Use each word once.

confirm	deceptive	defy	restrain
submit	susceptible	valid	vigorous

1. I gave the bottle such a _____ shake that it leaked Russian dressing all over my hands.

2. The dinosaur theory seemed _____ because all the available evidence supported it.

3. I don't go to the beach because I'm so _____ to sunburn.

4. At the party tonight, Nick will _____ he is engaged by introducing his date as "my fiancee."

5. In prison, the criminal had to _____ to more rules than he had ever thought possible.

6. Frankenstein's monster was so strong that even tying him down couldn't _____ him; he could escape whenever he wished.

7. "Looks can be _____," Ray's big brother warned. "Wendy may have a cute, childish face, but she's far from sweet."

8. The daring thief liked to openly _____ the police by leaving this note at the scene of the crime: "Love and Kisses from 'The Uncatchable One.'"

Now check your answers to these questions by turning to page 119. Going over the answers carefully will help you prepare for the next two checks, for which answers are not given.

➤ Sentence Check 2

Complete each sentence below with two words from the following list. Use each word once.

confirm	deceptive	defy	restrain
submit	susceptible	valid	vigorous

1-2. It took a _____ effort on the part of the police to _____ the angry mob from pushing through the gates.

3-4. Children who must _____ to overly strict rules often openly _____ their parents when they get older.

5-6. Buddy is so _____ to ear infections that he is never surprised to hear the

doctor _____ he has yet another one.

7-8. The title of the magazine article—"Miracle Weight Loss"—was _____. It suggested

there is a magical way to lose weight, but such a claim isn't _____—the facts show otherwise.

➤ Final Check: Chicken Pox

Here is a final opportunity for you to strengthen your knowledge of the eight words. First read the following passage carefully. Then fill in each blank with a word from the box at the top of this page. (Context clues will help you figure out which word goes in which blank.) Use each word once.

I remember the day my brother Danny dragged himself home from third grade and complained, "Mommy, I don't feel too good." My mother took one look at my usually (1)_____ brother, yelled "Aargh!" and flew up the stairs with him. The other eight of us ran after them, demanding to know what deadly disease he had. "Get away!" my mother cried. "It's chicken pox. You could catch it from him."

Poor Danny had to (2)_____ to having his spots checked by all the other mothers in the neighborhood. "Spots can be (3)_____," one lady explained. "They might have been measles, but I have to (4)_____ your mother's conclusion. These are definitely chicken pox."

After the women left, my mother said firmly, "None of you is to set foot in Danny's room for at least seven days. I don't think I could survive having the other eight of you sick all at once." She walked away muttering something about how it might already be too late because people are (5)_____ to chicken pox germs even before the sick person gets spots.

Then I started thinking: if my mother's claim that Danny's spots would last at least a week was (6)_____, that meant he would get out of school for a week. I was filled with jealousy. Still, I didn't want to (7)_____ my mother, so I didn't go to Danny's room during the forbidden seven days. Instead, unable to (8)_____ myself, I crawled into bed with him each night.

To this day, my mother says I purposely set out to destroy her sanity. But the situation wasn't all that bad. The eight of us didn't get sick all at once. The other seven got sick two weeks after me.

SCORES: Sentence Check 2 _____ %   **Final Check** _____ %
Enter your scores above and in the vocabulary performance chart on the inside back cover of the book.

Number right: 8 = 100%   7 = 88%   6 = 75%   5 = 63%   4 = 50%   3 = 38%   2 = 25%   1 = 13%

Previewing the Words

Find out how many of the eight words in this chapter you already know. Try to complete each sentence with the most suitable word from the list below. Use each word once.

Leave a sentence blank rather than guessing at an answer. Your purpose here is just to get a sense of the eight words and what you may know about them.

| accelerate | adverse | audible | coherent |
| comparable | competent | consecutive | deteriorate |

1. When two products are of _____ quality, why not buy the cheaper one?

2. The bank teller was known for being very _____—she did her job quickly and well.

3. When the microphone went dead, the lecturer's words were no longer _____ at the back of the hall.

4. Because of the _____ conditions of their first Arctic winter, many settlers returned to the comforts of civilization.

5. The singer's voice had not _____d at all during the course of her career. It was as strong, steady, and rich as ever.

6. The reporters would work nights for two _____ weeks, and then they'd work days for a month straight.

7. A good speech has a clear, _____ structure. That is, it is held together by logic and order.

8. Instead of slowing down at a yellow traffic light, Eric would _____ so that he could speed through before the light changed to red.

Now check your answers by turning to page 119. Fix any mistakes and fill in any blank spaces by writing in the correct answers. By doing so, you will complete this introduction to the eight words.

You're now ready to strengthen your knowledge of the words you already know and to master the words you're only half sure of, or don't know at all. Turn to the next page.

Eight Words in Context

Figure out the meanings of the following eight words by looking *closely and carefully* at the context in which the words appear. Doing so will prepare you for the matching test and the practices on the two pages that follow.

1 **accelerate**
(ak-sel'-ə-rāt')
-*verb*

    a. The sleds began sliding down the hill slowly and then **accelerated** to flying speed.

    b. Doug's car **accelerated** rapidly, allowing him to catch up with the slowly moving ice-cream truck.

2 **adverse**
(ad-vûrs')
-*adjective*

    a. Mozart created musical masterpieces in spite of his **adverse** circumstances—illness and debt.

    b. The **adverse** newspaper review of the last Marlon Brando movie convinced many readers not to see it.

3 **audible**
(ô'-də-bəl)
-*adjective*

    a. Dogs, bats, and other animals can hear high-pitched sounds that are not **audible** to humans.

    b. The argument next door was barely **audible**. So I put a cup on the wall and my ear to the cup so I could hear better.

4 **coherent**
(kō-hîr'-ənt)
-*adjective*

    a. To be sure that your essay has a **coherent** organization, write an outline first.

    b. Organizing ideas in a **coherent** manner on paper also helps one to think in a more orderly and logical way.

5 **comparable**
(kom'-pər-ə-bəl)
-*adjective*

    a. The quality of some relatively new used cars is **comparable** to that of brand-new ones.

    b. Because the two jobs were **comparable** in challenge, interest, and salary, Roy had trouble deciding which to take.

6 **competent**
(kom'-pi-tənt)
-*adjective*

    a. Some secretaries are more **competent** than their bosses. They know more about the business, are better organizers, and are much more hard-working.

    b. To be a **competent** juggler takes a lot of practice.

7 **consecutive**
(kən-sek'-yə-tiv)
-*adjective*

    a. Franklin Delano Roosevelt served three **consecutive** full terms as President and died not long after beginning his fourth.

    b. First Vera had the flu. That was immediately followed by mono, which was followed by pneumonia. These **consecutive** illnesses kept her out of work for two months.

8 **deteriorate**
(di-tîr'-ē-ə-rāt')
-*verb*

    a. Over many years, the abandoned house had **deteriorated** until its walls crumbled and its floorboards rotted.

    b. Jenny's health continued to **deteriorate** until her classmates started to visit her regularly. Then she began to improve.

Matching Words and Definitions

Check your understanding of the eight words by matching each word with its definition. Look back at the sentences in "Eight Words in Context" as needed to decide on the meaning of each word.

_____ 1. **accelerate**	a. able to be heard
_____ 2. **adverse**	b. following one after the other
_____ 3. **audible**	c. similar
_____ 4. **coherent**	d. harmful; unfavorable
_____ 5. **comparable**	e. to speed up
_____ 6. **competent**	f. connected in a logical and orderly way
_____ 7. **consecutive**	g. to become worse; go down in quality or condition
_____ 8. **deteriorate**	h. capable; well qualified

CAUTION: Do not go any further until you are sure the above answers are correct. If you have studied the "Eight Words in Context," you will know how to match each word. Then you can use the matches to help you in the following practices. Your goal is to reach a point where you don't need to check definitions at all.

➤*Sentence Check 1*

Complete each sentence below with the most suitable word from the box. Use each word once.

accelerate	adverse	audible	coherent
comparable	competent	consecutive	deteriorate

1. Anyone can become a _____ cook, but few people develop into great ones.

2. The summer's heat seemed endless. Records were set nationwide for the number of _____ days above ninety degrees.

3. When the comedian sensed his audience was becoming bored, he _____d his pace to more jokes per minute.

4. At the movies, Tina put her arm around me and said in a barely _____ whisper, "I love you. Pass the popcorn."

5. Our relationship began to _____ after we had a big fight over money.

6. People often bring their own children up in a manner _____ to the way they were raised. Thus abused children may become abusing parents.

7. During her high fever, Celia loudly called out broken words and phrases. She seemed unable to speak in full, _____ sentences.

8. The weather was bad, and two of the astronauts were sick. Because of these _____ conditions, the shuttle flight was canceled.

Now check your answers to these questions by turning to page 119. Going over the answers carefully will help you prepare for the next two checks, for which answers are not given.

➤ Sentence Check 2

Complete each sentence below with two words from the following list. Use each word once.

accelerate	adverse	audible	coherent
comparable	competent	consecutive	deteriorate

1-2. "Has your marriage started to _____?" asked the radio announcer. "If so, you may benefit from the services of Dr. Louis Frank, one of the city's most _____ marriage counselors."

3-4. Our neighbors have had parties this week on three _____ nights—on Friday, Saturday, and Sunday. And they played their stereo so loudly that it was _____ in our bedrooms.

5-6. The sun has an _____ effect on the skin. It _____s the aging of the skin, resulting in more wrinkles at a younger age.

7-8. We had trouble assembling the bike because the instructions were not _____ and we had to figure out the assembly on our own. Including such poorly written instructions is _____ to including none at all.

➤ Final Check: Walking

Here is a final opportunity for you to strengthen your knowledge of the eight words. First read the following passage carefully. Then fill in each blank with a word from the box at the top of this page. (Context clues will help you figure out which word goes in which blank.) Use each word once.

Walking and jogging are in no way (1)_____. Walking is very relaxing and can be done during all but the most (2)_____ outdoor conditions, such as icy sidewalks or a thunderstorm. Walking is also rather easy to learn; most people, in fact, are quite (3)_____ at it by their teens (but then they learn to drive, and the ability starts to (4)_____). Walkers see the world at a pleasantly leisurely rate. With each (5)_____ step, they take in another view of colorful flowers, beautiful trees, and collapsed joggers. In contrast, runners see the world as a blur of images jiggling up and down. Joggers bounce so much that passersby can't help but stare. Walkers, on the other hand, keep their pride. Unlike a runner, a walker needs to (6)_____ only if a growling dog appears nearby. Also, walkers can hold a conversation that is (7)_____ enough to make sense. In contrast, the jogger's brain is too shaken to produce orderly sentences, and the voice is reduced to a barely (8)_____ gasp. Certainly, walking is in every way superior to jogging. In walking, you just pass by. In jogging, you also pass out.

SCORES:	Sentence Check 2 _____ %		Final Check _____ %

Enter your scores above and in the vocabulary performance chart on the inside back cover of the book.

Number right: 8 = 100%   7 = 88%   6 = 75%   5 = 63%   4 = 50%   3 = 38%   2 = 25%   1 = 13%

UNIT FOUR: Test 1

PART A

Choose the word that best completes each sentence and write it in the space provided.

1. perceptive
   susceptible
   profound
   parallel

   Bernard is _____ to headaches. Whenever he has to study,

   his head starts to pound.

2. site
   vocation
   transaction
   destiny

   The land developer built a huge mall on the _____ where the

   racetrack had burned down.

3. data
   severity
   consequence
   severity

   Sharon feels she now has enough _____ to begin writing her

   report on eating disorders.

4. audible
   comparable
   valid
   parallel

   I have trouble parking _____ to the curb. My car is always

   farther out in back than in front.

5. competent
   theoretical
   deceptive
   conspicuous

   Instead of getting a _____ typist, my boss hired someone

   who types with one finger and usually hits the wrong key.

6. deteriorate
   defy
   dispense
   discriminate

   Doug bought orange socks instead of red because, in the store's poor lighting,

   he couldn't _____ between the two colors.

7. procrastinate
   diminish
   accelerate
   confirm

   Why doesn't crabgrass ever _____ ? Because every time

   you yank some out, you spread its seeds, causing more crabgrass to grow.

8. destiny
   severity
   site
   transaction

   Although buying a pair of panty hose seems like a minor _____,

   the customer gets about four miles of thread knitted into some three million
   loops.

9. defy
   submit
   accelerate
   confirm

   Vicky's children like to _____ her. No matter what she tells

   them to do, they'll do the opposite.

10. consecutive
    adverse
    comparable
    innate

    My English instructor has such high standards that a "B" from her is

    _____ to an "A" from most teachers.

(Continues on next page)

PART B
Circle **C** if the italicized word is used **correctly**. Circle **I** if the word is used **incorrectly**.

C I 11. The owl can hardly move its eyes. So the ability to turn its head nearly completely around is *vital* to its survival.

C I 12. I felt much worse when my muscle cramp *subsided*.

C I 13. My brother had to *restrain* himself to keep from eating the entire cheesecake.

C I 14. Angela's pregnancy made her so *vigorous* that all she wanted to do was sleep.

C I 15. I didn't realize the *severity* of Bill's injuries until I heard he was still in the hospital three months after his accident.

C I 16. My apartment is *dismal*. Several large windows allow the sun to shine in on the cheerful yellow and white furnishings.

C I 17. That survey was taken twenty years ago, so its findings probably aren't *valid* today.

C I 18. Gina *confirmed* the meeting time and place of her accounting class by looking in the college catalogue.

C I 19. When asked to pay for the window he had broken, Larry was *obstinate*. He said "Gladly!" and paid for it immediately.

C I 20. This summer, I'm taking an *accelerated* course that covers a full year's work in six weeks.

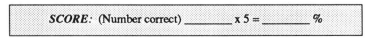

SCORE: (Number correct) _____ x 5 = _____ %

Enter your scores above and in the vocabulary performance chart on the inside back cover of the book.

UNIT FOUR: Test 2

PART A
Complete each sentence with a word from the box. Use each word once.

audible	deceptive	deteriorated	dispenses	innate
intervene	perceptive	procrastinate	submit	vocations

1. One server at the school cafeteria _____ larger portions than the others.

2. There's a club for people who like to ___procrastinate___. They haven't met yet because they keep postponing their first meeting.

3. I rarely _____ in fights between children. I believe they should work things out for themselves.

4. No one responded when the speaker asked, "Can you hear me?" because his words were too

    soft to be _____.

5. On Career Day, professionals came to the high school to tell the students about their

    ___vocations___.

6. I was shocked to see how my old high school has _____ since I moved away. It's in great need of repair.

7. The picture in the magazine ad is _____. It makes the doll look much larger than it really is.

8. My counselor is very _____. The other day she knew something was bothering me even though I said, "I'm fine."

9. Fred should never be put on a committee. He isn't willing to _____ to anyone else's suggestions.

10. My poor spelling ability must be ___perceptive___. I've had trouble with spelling ever since I started going to school.

(Continues on next page)

PART B
Circle **C** if the italicized word is used **correctly.** Circle **I** if the word is used **incorrectly.**

C I 11. Because so many of the rain forests are being destroyed, the *destiny* of many animals and insects may be to die out.

C I 12. We all thought the senator's speech was quite *coherent.* It was too disorganized to follow.

C I 13. Joyce's baby is more *sedate* than most. When he isn't climbing all over the furniture, he's screaming.

C I 14. Ruth is *morbid.* She always looks forward to a dance, a party, or dinner with a friend.

C I 15. Eric usually works every other weekend. But when he filled in for Ann on his weekend off, he ended up working three *consecutive* weekends.

C I 16. Early Latin American Indians had a *tedious* way of making the world's first sneakers. They simply dipped their feet into liquid rubber straight from the tree.

C I 17. A camel's hump stores fat that breaks down into water. As a *consequence,* a camel can survive for as long as two weeks without drinking.

C I 18. Today, those who walk or drive in the city are *detained* by stoplights and traffic. In the future, however, moving sidewalks may do away with the need for buses and cars in the city.

C I 19. The words of the song—"Yummy, yummy, yummy, I've got love in my tummy"—were so *profound* that I couldn't help laughing.

C I 20. I had to finish writing my report under *adverse* circumstances. It was late at night, the baby was crying, and my computer kept telling me it couldn't save what I had written.

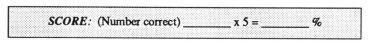

SCORE: (Number correct) _____ x 5 = _____ %

Enter your scores above and in the vocabulary performance chart on the inside back cover of the book.

UNIT FOUR: Test 3

PART A: Synonyms
In the space provided, write the letter of the choice that is most nearly the **same** in meaning as the boldfaced word.

_____ 1. **destiny**   a) delay   b) business deal   c) fate   d) hope

_____ 2. **obstinate**   a) discouraged   b) stubborn   c) calm   d) lively

_____ 3. **tedious**   a) inborn   b) neat   c) easy   d) boring

_____ 4. **parallel**   a) double   b) under   c) close   d) equally separated along a length

_____ 5. **restrain**   a) hold back   b) learn again   c) compare   d) aid

_____ 6. **intervene**   a) give in   b) harm   c) come between   d) entertain

_____ 7. **site**   a) action   b) location   c) speed   d) occupation

_____ 8. **transaction**   a) information   b) travel   c) difficulty   d) business exchange

_____ 9. **consecutive**   a) official   b) likely to be affected by   c) deep   d) one after the other

_____ 10. **morbid**   a) horrifying   b) additional   c) satisfying   d) expensive

_____ 11. **dispense**   a) distinguish   b) give out   c) disobey   d) keep

_____ 12. **susceptible**   a) unclear   b) necessary   c) sensitive   d) understanding

_____ 13. **detain**   a) send   b) delay   c) cooperate   d) train

_____ 14. **data**   a) information   b) cause   c) method   d) conclusion

_____ 15. **severity**   a) large numbers   b) seriousness   c) stubbornness   d) celebration

_____ 16. **procrastinate**   a) admire   b) support   c) accomplish   d) put off

_____ 17. **discriminate**   a) break   b) worsen   c) assist   d) distinguish

_____ 18. **profound**   a) deep   b) lost   c) uninteresting   d) simple

_____ 19. **vital**   a) discouraging   b) inborn   c) important   d) unavoidable

_____ 20. **perceptive**   a) disgusting   b) insightful   c) unemotional   d) energetic

(Continues on next page)

PART B: Antonyms
In the space provided, write the letter of the choice that is most nearly the **opposite** in meaning to the boldfaced word.

_____21. **diminish**   a) increase   b) keep   c) know   d) forbid

_____22. **consequence**   a) explanation   b) membership   c) time   d) cause

_____23. **comparable**   a) free   b) different   c) available   d) known

_____24. **deteriorate**   a) improve   b) offer   c) worsen   d) claim

_____25. **competent**   a) late   b) angry   c) unskilled   d) calm

_____26. **accelerate**   a) plan   b) admit   c) require   d) slow down

_____27. **deceptive**   a) logical   b) truthful   c) skillful   d) lively

_____28. **coherent**   a) disconnected   b) boring   c) frightening   d) deep

_____29. **innate**   a) stiff   b) unclear   c) inborn   d) learned

_____30. **subside**   a) lean   b) increase   c) please   d) avoid

_____31. **defy**   a) lift   b) recognize   c) obey   d) look

_____32. **sedate**   a) hidden   b) tight   c) excited   d) sudden

_____33. **submit**   a) own   b) resist   c) forget   d) gather

_____34. **confirm**   a) deny   b) compete   c) win   d) clean up

_____35. **dismal**   a) unusual   b) cheerful   c) dull   d) modest

_____36. **vocation**   a) hobby   b) job   c) pay   d) barrier

_____37. **valid**   a) difficult   b) illogical   c)easy   d) long

_____38. **audible**   a) nearby   b) not able to be heard   c) able to be seen   d) logical

_____39. **adverse**   a) ready   b) colorful   c) favorable   d) well-known

_____40. **vigorous**   a) early   b) misleading   c) not alike   d) weak

_____
| *SCORE:* (Number correct) _____ x 2.5 = _____ % |
_____

Enter your scores above and in the vocabulary performance chart on the inside back cover of the book.

UNIT FOUR: Test 4

PART A

Complete each sentence in a way that clearly shows you understand the meaning of the boldfaced word. Take a minute to plan your answer before you write.

Example: A child might **defy** a parent by _____ *refusing to mow the lawn.* _____

1. A camper might experience such **adverse** conditions as _____

2. One **valid** reason for missing class is _____

3. I usually **accelerate** my car when _____

4. Ramon felt **dismal** because _____

5. One especially **tedious** activity is _____

6. I often **procrastinate** when _____

7. You could **confirm** a date with a friend by _____

8. Babies have an **innate** ability to _____

9. If you were to **submit** to someone's demand for a loan, you would _____

10. To achieve my career goals, it is **vital** that I _____

(Continues on next page)

PART B

After each boldfaced word are a *synonym* (a word that means the same as the boldfaced word), an *antonym* (a word that means the opposite of the boldfaced word), and a word that is neither. Mark the synonym with an *S* and the antonym with an *A*.

Example: **inept**	_____ common	__*A*__ skilled	__*S*__ clumsy
11-12. **vigorous**	__*S*__ energetic	_____ inexpensive	__*A*__ weak
13-14. **competent**	_____ peaceful	_____ unqualified	_____ capable
15-16. **subside**	_____ examine	_____ lessen	_____ increase
17-18. **sedate**	_____ lively	_____ gloomy	_____ calm
19-20. **obstinate**	_____ flexible	_____ stubborn	_____ intelligent

PART C

Use five of the following ten words in sentences. Make it clear that you know the meaning of the word you use. Feel free to use the past tense or plural form of a word.

audible	comparable	consequence	deteriorate	intervene
perceptive	profound	severity	subside	vocation

21. _____

_____

22. _____

_____

23. _____

_____

24. _____

_____

25. _____

SCORE: (Number correct) _____ x 4 = _____ %

Enter your scores above and in the vocabulary performance chart on the inside back cover of the book.

A. Limited Answer Key

An Important Note: Be sure to use this answer key as a learning tool only. You should not turn to this key until you have considered carefully the sentence in which a given word appears.

Used properly, the key will help you to learn words and to prepare for the activities and tests for which answers are not given. For ease of reference, the title of the "Final Check" passage in each chapter appears in parentheses.

Chapter 1 (Taking Exams)

Previewing the Words

1. drastic
2. candid
3. comply
4. acknowledge
5. appropriate
6. alternative
7. compel
8. concise

Sentence Check 1

1. candid
2. drastic
3. concise
4. comply
5. compel
6. alternative
7. acknowledge
8. appropriate

Chapter 2 (Nate the Woodsman)

Previewing the Words

1. urban
2. erratic
3. fortify
4. reminisce
5. extensive
6. illuminate
7. isolate
8. refuge

Sentence Check 1

1. erratic
2. refuge
3. fortify
4. isolate
5. reminisce
6. illuminate
7. extensive
8. urban

Chapter 3 (Who's on Trial?)

Previewing the Words

1. legitimate
2. morale
3. menace
4. undermine
5. lenient
6. naive
7. impartial
8. overt

Sentence Check 1

1. impartial
2. undermine
3. menace
4. morale
5. legitimate
6. naive
7. overt
8. lenient

Chapter 4 (Night Nurse)

Previewing the Words

1. illusion
2. novice
3. hypocrite
4. obstacle
5. idealistic
6. endorse
7. impact
8. imply

Sentence Check 1

1. imply
2. novice
3. idealistic
4. hypocrite
5. endorse
6. impact
7. obstacle
8. illusion

Chapter 5 (Relating to Parents)

Previewing the Words

1. concede
2. scapegoat
3. transition
4. superficial
5. conservative
6. sustain
7. denounce
8. deter

Sentence Check 1

1. scapegoat
2. sustain
3. denounce
4. concede
5. deter
6. superficial
7. transition
8. conservative

Chapter 6 (Job Choices)

Previewing the Words

1. surpass
2. tentative
3. compensate
4. derive
5. supplement
6. moderate
7. verify
8. diversity

Sentence Check 1

1. derive
2. verify
3. moderate
4. tentative
5. surpass
6. supplement
7. diversity
8. compensate

Chapter 7 (Museum Pet)

Previewing the Words

1. prominent
2. prudent
3. donor
4. acute
5. recipient
6. anonymous
7. arrogant
8. apprehensive

Sentence Check 1

1. anonymous
2. acute
3. arrogant
4. recipient
5. prudent
6. apprehensive
7. donor
8. prominent

Chapter 8 (My Headstrong Baby)

Previewing the Words

1. rational	5. awe
2. accessible	6. exempt
3. prevail	7. retort
4. retrieve	8. cite

Sentence Check 1

1. prevail	5. accessible
2. retrieve	6. cite
3. exempt	7. rational
4. awe	8. retort

Chapter 9 (A Narrow Escape)

Previewing the Words

1. obsession	5. elapse
2. fluent	6. evasive
3. ordeal	7. persistent
4. infer	8. lethal

Sentence Check 1

1. fluent	5. lethal
2. obsession	6. ordeal
3. evasive	7. persistent
4. elapse	8. infer

Chapter 10 (The Power of Advertising)

Previewing the Words

1. versatile	5. convey
2. subtle	6. stimulate
3. savor	7. devise
4. vivid	8. unique

Sentence Check 1

1. devise	5. stimulate
2. savor	6. convey
3. subtle	7. unique
4. vivid	8. versatile

Chapter 11 (Waiter)

Previewing the Words

1. equate	5. inevitable
2. endeavor	6. impose
3. patron	7. indignant
4. option	8. passive

Sentence Check 1

1. inevitable	5. patron
2. option	6. impose
3. equate	7. indignant
4. passive	8. endeavor

Chapter 12 (Adjusting to a New Culture)

Previewing the Words

1. retain	5. gesture
2. reciprocate	6. refuted
3. dismay	7. exile
4. ritual	8. adapt

Sentence Check 1

1. dismay	5. adapt
2. refute	6. exile
3. gesture	7. reciprocate
4. retain	8. ritual

Chapter 13 (A Dream About Wealth)

Previewing the Words

1. frugal	5. notable
2. elaborate	6. exotic
3. mediocre	7. indifferent
4. emerge	8. liberal

Sentence Check 1

1. mediocre	5. elaborate
2. emerge	6. frugal
3. notable	7. indifferent
4. liberal	8. exotic

Chapter 14 (Children and Drugs)

Previewing the Words

1. coerce	5. affirm
2. query	6. sadistic
3. impair	7. elite
4. essence	8. allude

Sentence Check 1

1. coerce	5. affirm
2. sadistic	6. elite
3. impair	7. query
4. essence	8. allude

Chapter 15 (Party House)

Previewing the Words

1. revoke	5. reprimand
2. recur	6. shrewd
3. tactic	7. plausible
4. skeptical	8. stereotype

Sentence Check 1

1. stereotype	5. tactic
2. plausible	6. skeptical
3. shrewd	7. reprimand
4. recur	8. revoke

Chapter 16 (Procrastinator)

Previewing the Words

1. vital
2. consequence
3. procrastinate
4. detain
5. transaction
6. destiny
7. diminish
8. Tedious

Sentence Check 1

1. transaction
2. diminish
3. procrastinate
4. consequence
5. destiny
6. vital
7. detain
8. tedious

Chapter 17 (Changes in View)

Previewing the Words

1. vocation
2. severity
3. subside
4. site
5. profound
6. dispense
7. discriminate
8. dismal

Sentence Check 1

1. discriminate
2. profound
3. subside
4. vocation
5. dismal
6. dispense
7. severity
8. site

Chapter 18 (Family Differences)

Previewing the Words

1. obstinate
2. Perceptive
3. data
4. morbid
5. intervene
6. innate
7. parallel
8. sedate

Sentence Check 1

1. data
2. morbid
3. sedate
4. perceptive
5. parallel
6. intervene
7. obstinate
8. innate

Chapter 19 (Chicken Pox)

Previewing the Words

1. valid
2. confirm
3. defy
4. submit
5. susceptible
6. restrain
7. deceptive
8. vigorous

Sentence Check 1

1. vigorous
2. valid
3. susceptible
4. confirm
5. submit
6. restrain
7. deceptive
8. defy

Chapter 20 (Walking)

Previewing the Words

1. comparable
2. competent
3. audible
4. adverse
5. deteriorate
6. consecutive
7. coherent
8. accelerate

Sentence Check 1

1. competent
2. consecutive
3. accelerate
4. audible
5. deteriorate
6. comparable
7. coherent
8. adverse

B. Dictionary Use

It isn't always possible to figure out the meaning of a word from its context, and that's where a dictionary comes in. Following is some basic information to help you use a dictionary.

HOW TO FIND A WORD

A dictionary contains so many words that it can take a while to find the one you're looking for. But if you know how to use guide words, you can find a word rather quickly. *Guide words* are the two words at the top of each dictionary page. The first guide word tells what the first word is on the page. The second guide word tells what the last word is on that page. The other words on a page fall alphabetically between the two guide words. So when you look up a word, find the two guide words that alphabetically surround the word you're looking for.

• Which of the following pair of guide words would be on a page with the word *skirmish*?

   skimp/ skyscraper   **skyward / slave**   **sixty / skimming**

The answer to this question and the ones that follow are given on the next page.

HOW TO USE A DICTIONARY LISTING

A dictionary listing includes many pieces of information. For example, here is a listing from the *Random House College Dictionary*, Paperback Edition. Note that it includes much more than just a definition.

   driz·zle (driz'əl), *v.*, **-zled, -zling,** *n.* —*v.* **1.** to rain gently and steadily in fine drops. — *n.* **2.** a very light rain. —**driz'zly,** *adj.*

Key parts of a dictionary entry are listed and explained below.

Syllables. Dots separate dictionary entry words into syllables. Note that *drizzle* has one dot, which breaks the word into two syllables.

• To practice seeing the syllable breakdown in a dictionary entry, write the number of syllables in each word below.

   gla·mour _____   **mic·ro·wave** _____   **in·de·scrib·a·ble** _____

Pronunciation guide. The information within parentheses after the entry word shows how to pronounce the entry word. This pronunciation guide includes two types of symbols: pronunciation symbols and accent marks.

Pronunciation symbols represent the consonant and vowel sounds in a word. The consonant sounds are probably very familiar to you, but you may find it helpful to review some of the sounds of the vowels—*a, e, i, o,* and *u.* Every dictionary has a key explaining the sounds of its pronunciation symbols, including the long and short sounds of vowels.

Long vowels have the sound of their own names. For example, the *a* in *pay* and the *o* in *no* both have long vowel sounds. Long vowel sounds are shown by a line above the vowel.

In the *Random House College Dictionary*, the *short vowels* are shown by the use of the vowel itself, with no other markings. Thus the *i* in the first syllable of *drizzle* is a short *i*. What do the short vowels sound like? Below are words from the *RHCD* pronunciation key which illustrate the *short vowel* sounds.

   a bat   **e** set   **i** big   **o** box   **u** up

This key means, for example, that the *a* in *bat* has the short-*a* sound.

- Which of the words below has a short vowel sound? Which has a long vowel sound?

  drug _____   **night** _____   **sand** _____

Another pronunciation symbol is the *schwa*, which looks like an upside-down *e*. It stands for certain rapidly spoken, unaccented vowel sounds, such as the *a* in *above*, the *e* in *item*, the *i* in *easily*, the *o* in *gallop*, and the *u* in *circus*. Here are three words that include the schwa sound:

  in·fant (in'fənt)   **bum·ble** (bum'bəl)   **de·liv·er** (di-liv'ər)

- Which syllable in *drizzle* contains the schwa sound, the first or the second? _____

Accent marks are small black marks that tell you which syllable to emphasize, or stress, as you say a word. An accent mark follows *driz* in the pronunciation guide for *drizzle*, which tells you to stress the first syllable of *drizzle*. Syllables with no accent mark are not stressed. Some syllables are in between, and they are marked with a lighter accent mark.

- Which syllable has the stronger accent in *sentimental*? _____

  sen·ti·men·tal (sen'tə-men'tl)

Parts of Speech. After the pronunciation key and before each set of definitions, the entry word's parts of speech are given. The parts of speech are abbreviated as follows:

  noun—*n.*   pronoun—*pron.*   adjective—*adj.*   adverb—*adv.*   verb—*v.*

- The listing for *drizzle* shows it has two parts of speech. Write them below:

  _____   _____

Definitions. Words often have more than one meaning. When they do, each meaning is usually numbered in the dictionary. You can tell which definition of a word fits a given sentence by the meaning of the sentence. For example, the word *charge* has several definitions, including these two: **1.** to ask as a price. **2.** to accuse or blame.

- Show with a check which definition applies in each sentence below:

  The store charged me less for the blouse because it was missing a button.   1 ___   2 ___

  My neighbor has been charged with shoplifting.   1 ___   2 ___

Other Information. After the definitions in a listing in a hardbound dictionary, you may get information about the *origin* of a word. Such information about origins, also known as *etymology*, is usually given in brackets. And you may sometimes be given one or more synonyms or antonyms for the entry word. *Synonyms* are words that are similar in meaning to the entry word; *antonyms* are words that are opposite in meaning.

WHICH DICTIONARIES TO OWN

You will find it useful to own two recent dictionaries: a small paperback dictionary to carry to class and a hardbound dictionary, which contains more information than a small paperback one. Among the good dictionaries strongly recommended are both the paperback and hardcover editions of the following:

  The Random House College Dictionary
  The American Heritage Dictionary
  Webster's New World Dictionary

ANSWERS TO THE DICTIONARY QUESTIONS

Guide words: *skimp/skyscraper*
Number of syllables: 2, 3, 5
Vowels: *drug, sand* (short); *night* (long)
Schwa: second syllable of *drizzle*

Accent: stronger accent on third syllable
Parts of speech: noun and verb
Definitions: 1; 2

C. Word List

accelerate, 105
accessible, 41
acknowledge, 5
acute, 37
adapt, 65
adverse, 105
affirm, 73
allude, 73
alternative, 5
anonymous, 37
apprehensive, 37
appropriate, 5
arrogant, 37
audible, 105
awe, 41
candid, 5
cite, 41
coerce, 73
coherent, 105
comparable, 105
compel, 5
compensate, 33
competent, 105
comply, 5
concede, 21
concise, 5
confirm, 101
consecutive, 105
consequence, 89
conservative, 21
convey, 49
data, 97
deceptive, 101
defy, 101
denounce, 21
derive, 33
destiny, 89
detain, 89
deter, 21
deteriorate, 105
devise, 49
diminish, 89
discriminate, 93
dismal, 93
dismay, 65

dispense, 93
diversity, 33
donor, 37
drastic, 5
elaborate, 69
elapse, 45
elite, 73
emerge, 69
endeavor, 61
endorse, 17
equate, 61
erratic, 9
essence, 73
evasive, 45
exempt, 41
exile, 65
exotic, 69
extensive, 9
fluent, 45
fortify, 9
frugal, 69
gesture, 65
hypocrite, 17
idealistic, 17
illuminate, 9
illusion, 17
impact, 17
impair, 73
impartial, 13
imply, 17
impose, 61
indifferent, 69
indignant, 61
inevitable, 61
infer, 45
innate, 97
intervene, 97
isolate, 9
legitimate, 13
lenient, 13
lethal, 45
liberal, 69
mediocre, 69
menace, 13
moderate, 33

morale, 13
morbid, 97
naive, 13
notable, 69
novice, 17
obsession, 45
obstacle, 17
obstinate, 97
option, 61
ordeal, 45
overt, 13
parallel, 97
passive, 61
patron, 61
perceptive, 97
persistent, 45
plausible, 77
prevail, 41
procrastinate, 89
profound, 93
prominent, 37
prudent, 37
query, 73
rational, 41
recipient, 37
reciprocate, 65
recur, 77
refuge, 9
refute, 65
reminisce, 9
reprimand, 77
restrain, 101
retain, 65
retort, 41
retrieve, 41
revoke, 77
ritual, 65
sadistic, 73
savor, 49
scapegoat, 21
sedate, 97
severity, 93
shrewd, 77
site, 93
skeptical, 77

stereotype, 77
stimulate, 49
submit, 101
subside, 93
subtle, 49
superficial, 21
supplement, 33
surpass, 33
susceptible, 101
sustain, 21
tactic, 77
tedious, 89
tentative, 33
transaction, 89
transition, 21
undermine, 13
unique, 49
urban, 9
valid, 101
verify, 33
versatile, 49
vigorous, 101
vital, 89
vivid, 49
vocation, 93